D0297648

Wesley Country

Behind 'Wesley Country'

RICHARD BEWES, compiler of Wesley Country, is a product of East African missionary parents, a graduate of Cambridge University and a London Preacher. He had completed twenty years as Rector of All Souls Church, Langham Place by early 2003. His books, and his hosting - with All Souls colleague Paul Blackham - of the international video and television courses Open Home, Open Bible and Book by Book are meeting with a response in many countries.

With a grandfather converted to Christ through the American Evangelist D.L. Moody, and having known and worked with Dr and Mrs Billy Graham over many years, evangelism and world mission are at the front of Richard Bewes' vision. Hence his longstanding interest in John Wesley - for the Wesley brothers, he maintains, have always been bigger than Methodism itself. The Wesleys were the spiritual forefathers of the anti-slave trade campaigner William Wilberforce and the group of Anglican Evangelical reformers at Holy Trinity Church Clapham, known popularly as The Clapham Sect.

Richard Bewes declares, 'The Great movements for world evangelism have never sprung from appointed committees. In any generation a flame can be lit in the heart of an individual; a Wesley, a Whitefield, a Hannah Moore or an Ashley Cooper… and society feels the difference. Then - as at the time of the Clapham Sect - the breathtaking realisation breaks surface, Our church could touch the world.

Three hundred years after the birth of John Wesley, we, the publishers, Gerald Thompson and Robert Hicks, dare to hope - in company with our compiler - that these pages will put new heart into those reaching out to a dying world through the printed page, Internet, media, including Radio and Television, satellite communication and the direct proclaiming of God's Holy Word. It was Wesley who showed us the way in his phrase

The World is My Parish.

Wesley Country

A Pictorial History
based on John Wesley's Journal

Compiled by Richard Bewes

Published by Bible Matters with Creative Publishing

50, St Lawrence Avenue, Worthing, West Sussex, BN14 7JG

Acknowledgements:

Concept: Robert Hicks

Editor: Richard Bewes

Picture research: Richard Bewes

Historical research: Richard Bewes

Art Editor: Roger Chouler

Calligraphy: Elaine Cooper

Design: Richard Bewes

　　　　Elaine Cooper

　　　　Robert Hicks

　　　　Roger Chouler

Cover and prelims of this edition designed by Kevin Raddy

Copyright © 2003 Creative Publishing.

Published by Bible Matters, Worthing, England.

All rights reserved. No part of this book may be reproduced, stored in a retreval system,
or transmitted in any form or by any means, electronic, mechanical, photocopying,
recording, or otherwise, without the written permission of the publishers.

ISBN: 1-904636-01-2

Printed in India

Contents

Introduction

ONE COLD ENGLISH NIGHT, in February 1709, the old parsonage at Epworth, in Lincolnshire went up in flames. The Reverend Samuel Wesley and his wife Susanna brought their family out into the garden, only to discover that their fifteenth and youngest child, 'Jacky', was still in the house. On hurrying inside to rescue the five-year old, Samuel found his way blocked at the foot of the stairs by a wall of roaring flame and choking smoke - upon which he 'knelt down in the blazing hall and commended the soul of his child to God.'

But then help came, as a rescuer, standing on the shoulders of another, reached up to the first floor window and grabbed the little boy to safety. In later years John Wesley was to describe himself as 'a brand plucked out of the burning.' The phrase aptly illustrated the Gospel urgency that was to touch the preaching of England's most effective evangelist ever - whose own heart was 'strangely warmed' in London's Aldersgate Street on May 24th, 1738.

Born on June 17th, 1703, it has been well argued that Wesley's was the most celebrated and productive life in the whole of the eighteenth century. Evangelising the length and breadth of the British Isles with his hymn-writing brother Charles, it may fairly be claimed that England was spared the fires of the French Revolution as the preaching of the Wesleys took hold.

John Wesley has an honoured place in the long parade of Gospel preachers. He and his contemporary George Whitefield must be ranked alongside Irenaeus of Lyons, the 'golden- mouthed' John Chrysostom of Constantinople in the fourth century, Patrick of Ireland, Francis of Assisi, Wycliffe, Bunyan, Kate Booth of the Salvation Army, D.L. Moody of Chicago and Billy Graham of Montreat, North Carolina.

Certainly Wesley was the most travelled individual of his own day, having covered in all the equivalent of ten times round the world (mostly on horseback). It is estimated that in all his travels with his hymn-writing brother Charles Wesley, he had preached no less than forty thousand sermons.

In these pages, Wesley is allowed to speak for himself, in the clear direct style of his long-distant running Journal. The arrangement is geographical rather than chronological; so we observe the evangelist against a variety of regional and sociological backgrounds. In this way we can see how the man and his age are related, and the wideness of his mission appreciated - for John Wesley has been a burning and shining light across three hundred years.

RICHARD BEWES
Written at All Souls Church, Langham Place,
London, 2003.

A New Map of ENGLAND, SCOTLAND and IRELAND

REPRODUCED FROM
AN ORIGINAL EIGHTEENTH-
CENTURY MAP

OXFORD

OXFORD – the name points to a ford for oxen across the Thames – stood originally, as a late Saxon –planned town, on a low gravel ridge between the Thames and its tributary, the Cherwell. The chief stronghold in the upper Thames valley, Oxford had sustained various attacks by the Danes at the turn of the tenth century, and was to develop as a prosperous borough long before the birth of the university through the influence of Dominican and Franciscan friars.

AN OLD PRINT OF OXFORD

By Wesley's time the abbeys and friars' churches of Oxford had long been swept away by the Reformation, and the city had acquired a political flavour, having been the headquarters of the Royalist party during the Civil War. The restoration was to lead to conflicts between students and citizens, and Jacobite riots broke out in the reign of George I. Nevertheless Wesley retained a love of the city with its colleges, towers, spires and water-meadows – a peerless city.

GATEWAY OF ST. MARY'S CHURCH, OXFORD

1738

ARMS OF THE CITY AND UNIVERSITY OF OXFORD

JOHN WESLEY, FELLOW OF LINCOLN COLLEGE, OXFORD

Saturday, March 4 — I found my brother at Oxford, recovering from his pleurisy; and with him Peter Böhler; by whom (in the hands of the great God) I was, on Sunday, the 5th, clearly convinced of unbelief, of the want of that faith whereby alone we are saved.

Immediately it struck into my mind, "Leave off preaching. How can you preach to others, who have not faith yourself?" I asked Böhler whether he thought I should leave it off or not. He answered, "By no means." I asked, "But what can I preach?" He said, "Preach faith till you have it; and then, because you have it, you will preach faith." Accordingly, Monday 6, I began preaching this new doctrine, though my soul started back from this work. The first person to whom I offered salvation by faith alone, was a prisoner under sentence of death. His name was Clifford. Peter Böhler had many times desired me to speak to him before. But I could not prevail on myself so to do; being still (as I had been many years a zealous asserter of the impossibility of a death-bed repentance.

1744 Friday, August 24 (St. Bartholomew's Day) — I preached, I suppose the last time, at St. Mary's. Be it so. I am now clear of the blood of these men. I have fully delivered my own soul.

The beadle came to me afterwards, and told me the Vice-Chancellor had sent him for my notes. I sent them without delay, not without admiring the wise providence of God. Perhaps few men of note would have given a sermon of mine the reading, if I had put it into their hands; but by this means it came to be read, probably more than once, by every man of eminence in the university.

1778 Wednesday, October 14 – I went on to Oxford, and, having an hour to spare, walked to Christ-church, for which I cannot but still retain a peculiar affection. What lovely mansions are these! What is wanting to make the inhabitants of them happy? That, without which no rational creature can be happy - the experimental know-

ledge of God. In the evening I preached at Finstock, to a congregation gathered from many miles around. How gladly could I spend a few weeks in this delightful solitude! But I must not rest yet. As long as God gives me strength to labour, I am to use it.

1782 Tuesday, October 15 — About noon I preached at Oxford. I have seen no such prospect here for many years. The congregation was large and still as night, although many gentlemen were among them. The next evening the house would not contain the congregation; yet all were quiet, even those that could not come in: and I believe God not only opened their understandings, but began a good work in some of their hearts.

BOCARDO PRISON, OXFORD

1783 Monday, July 14 – In the evening I preached in the new preaching-house at Oxford, a lightsome, cheerful place, and well-filled with rich and poor, scholars as well as townsmen.

Tuesday, July 15 – Walking through the city I observed it swiftly improving in everything but religion. Observing narrowly the hall at Christ-church, I was convinced it is both loftier and larger than that of the Stadt-house

OXFORD FROM HEADINGTON HILL, A TOWN OF TOWERS AND SPIRES

CHRIST CHURCH, OXFORD, IN THE 16TH CENTURY

in Amsterdam. I observed also, the gardens and walks in Holland, although extremely pleasant, were not to be compared with St. John's or Trinity gardens; much less with the parks, Magdalen water-walks etc., Christ-church meadow, or the White-walk.

ENTRANCE TO THE BOTANICAL GARDENS, OXFORD

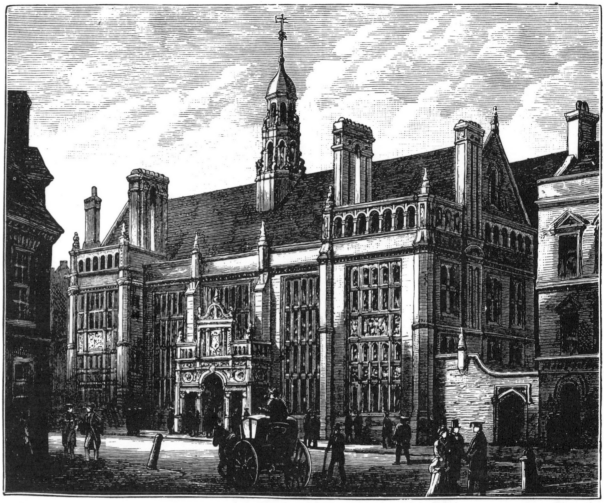

THE NEW SCHOOLS, OXFORD

' They always took me to be a little crack-brained at Oxford.'

Journals, July 17, 1739

LONDON

ST. PAUL'S CATHEDRAL, LONDON

LONDON (Aldersgate, Islington, Blackheath, Wapping, Kennington). 'When a man is tired of London he is tired of life,' wrote one of the metropolis' most celebrated devotees, Dr. Johnson, in 1777. For all the brilliance of the Empire's capital, however, London of the eighteenth century represented a mass of inequalities and contradictory values.

The population was to increase during the century from 674,000 to around the million mark, but, around 1735, three quarters of all the children baptised were dying under the age of five. Disease, the workhouse and, perhaps above all, the curse of gin, were to take their toll, London being the centre of England's distilling industry. The year before John Wesley was born, Daniel Defoe wrote, 'An honest drunken fellow is a character in a man's praise.' Even by the middle of the century it was estimated that in Holborn one house in five sold spirits.

The age was one of coarseness and brutality. All of London would turn out on Mondays for the Tyburn hangings. Bishop Butler (1692-1752) summed up the current spirit of retreating morals and arid unbelief when he wrote, 'It has come to be taken for granted that Christianity is not so much a subject for enquiry, but that it is now at length discovered to be fictitious.' But it was the darkest hour before the dawn. 1738 marked the turning point in John Wesley's life, one Wednesday in May in Aldersgate Street. A flame was lit that evening in London which was to sweep the entire nation.

DR. SAMUEL JOHNSON

ISLINGTON IN THE 18TH CENTURY

1738 Wednesday, May 24 – In the evening I went very unwillingly to a society in Aldersgate-Street, where one was reading Luther's preface to the Epistle to the Romans. About a quarter before nine, while he was describing the change which God works in the heart through faith in Christ, I felt my heart strangely warmed. I felt I did trust in Christ, Christ alone, for salvation; and an assurance was given me, that He had taken away my sins, even mine, and saved me from the law of sin and death.

Thursday, May 25 – The moment I awakened "Jesus, Master," was in my heart and in my mouth; and I found, all my

GEORGE WHITEFIELD

strength lay in keeping my eye fixed upon Him, and my soul waiting on Him continually.

1739 Wednesday, June 13 - In the morning I came to London; and after receiving the Holy Communion at Islington, I had once more the opportunity of seeing my mother, whom I had not seen since my return from Germany.

Thursday, June 14 — I went with Mr. Whitefield to Blackheath, where were, I believe, twelve or fourteen thousand people. He a little surprised me, by desiring me to preach in his stead; which I did (though nature recoiled) on my favourite subject: "Jesus Christ, Who of God is made unto us wisdom, righteousness, sanctification and redemption." I was greatly moved with compassion for the rich that were there, to whom I made a particular application. Some of them seemed to attend, while others drove away their coaches from so uncouth a preacher.

Friday, June 15 — I went to a society at Wapping, weary in body and faint in spirit . . . . While I was earnestly inviting all sinners to "enter into the holiest" by this new and living way, many of those that heard began to call upon God with strong cries and tears. Some sunk down, and there remained no strength in them; others exceedingly trembled and quaked; some were torn with a kind of convulsive motion in every part of their bodies, and that so violently, that often four or five persons could not hold one of them. I have seen many hysterical and many epileptic fits; but none of them were like these, in many respects. I immediately prayed that God would not suffer those who were weak to be offended.

Saturday, June 17 — I preached, at seven, in Upper Moorfields, to (I believe) six or seven thousand people, on: "Ho! everyone that thirsteth, come ye to the waters!" At five I preached on Kennington Common, to people from "all the ends of the earth."

KENSINGTON GARDENS, LONDON, IMPROVED BY CAROLINE, WIFE OF GEORGE II, IN THE 18TH CENTURY

KENNINGTON

want of love was a general complaint. We laid it open before our Lord. We soon found He had sent us an answer of peace. Evil surmisings vanished away. The flame kindled again as at the first, and our hearts were knit together.

Tuesday, 18 – A young woman (Nanny Smith) came to see us at Islington in such an agony as I have seldom seen. Her sorrow and fear were too big for utterance; so that, after a few words, her strength as well as her heart failing, she sunk down to the ground. Only her sighs and her groans showed she was yet alive. We cried unto God in her behalf. We claimed the promises made to the weary and heavy-laden; and He did not cast out our prayer. She saw her Saviour as it were crucified before her eyes. She laid hold on Him by faith, and her spirit revived.

Sunday, September 9 — I declared to about ten thousand, in Moorfields, what they must do to be saved. My mother went with us, about five, to Kennington, where were supposed to be twenty thousand people. I again insisted on that foundation of all our hope: "Believe in the Lord Jesus, and thou shalt be saved." From Kennington I went to a society at Lambeth. The house being filled, the rest stood in the garden. The deep attention they showed gave me a good hope, that they will not all be forgetful hearers.

Thence I went to our society at Fetter-lane, and exhorted them to love one another. The

THE THAMES EMBANKMENT

LINCOLNSHIRE EPWORTH

EPWORTH CHURCH

EPWORTH, which features in Domesday, was notable for its most famous son, John Wesley, the fifteenth child of Samuel and Susanna Wesley, born at Epworth Rectory on June 17th, 1703. The rectory was burnt down on February 9th, 1709, and the children escaped narrowly. Wesley was to return to the scene of his father's labours many times during his itinerant ministry.

Alfred the Great celebrated his marriage with Ealswitha at the Lincolnshire town of Gainsborough; otherwise there are few historical references to this, the second-largest county in England, before the Danish invasion made its permanent mark on place names and dialect alike. William the Conqueror was to build a castle at Lincoln, distributing the main estates among his Norman followers; but in general the Domesday Survey reveals that the county was leniently treated. The city of Lincoln has a rich inheritance of Norman architecture, its crowning glory centering in its superb cathedral, first consecrated on May 6th, 1092. The county was to witness the growth of maritime and fishing towns, notably Boston, Grimsby, Barton, Saltfleet, Wainfleet and Wrangle. The early manufactures of the county are all connected with the woollen trade.

1742 Saturday June 5 — I rode for Epworth. It being many years since I had been in Epworth before, I went to an inn, in the middle of the town, not knowing whether there were any left in it now who would not be ashamed of my acquaintance. But an old servant of my father's, with two or three poor women, presently found me out. I asked her, "Do you know any in Epworth who are in earnest to be saved?" She answered, "I am, by the grace of God; and I know I am saved through faith . . ."

Sunday, June 6 — A little before the service began, I went to Mr. Romley, the curate, and offered to assist him either by preaching or reading prayers. But he did not care to accept of my assistance. The church

WESLEY PREACHING ON HIS FATHER'S TOMB

KINGSTON-UPON-HULL

was exceeding full in the afternoon, a rumour being spread that I was to preach. But the sermon on: "Quench not the Spirit," was not suitable to the expectation of many of the hearers. Mr. Romley told them, one of the most dangerous ways of quenching the Spirit was by enthusiasm; and enlarged on the character of an enthusiast, in a very florid and oratorical manner. After the sermon John Taylor stood in the churchyard, and gave notice, as the people were coming out, "Mr. Wesley, not being permitted to preach in the church, designs to preach here at six o'clock."

Accordingly at six I came, and found such a congregation as I believe Epworth never saw before. I stood near the east end of the church upon my father's tombstone, and cried: "The kingdom of heaven is not meat and drink; but righteousness, and peace, and joy in the Holy Ghost."

Sunday, June 13 — At six I preached for the last time in Epworth churchyard, (being to leave the town the next morning,) to a vast multitude gathered together from all parts, on the beginning of our Lord's Sermon on the Mount. I continued among them for near three hours; and yet we scarce knew how to part. O let none think his labour of love is lost because the fruit does not immediately appear! Near forty years did my father labour here; but he saw little fruit of all his labour...

"A GENTLEWOMAN INVITED MY WIFE AND ME TO COME INTO HER COACH."

1752 Friday, April 24 — When I landed at the quay in Hull, it was covered with people, inquiring, "Which is he? Which is he?" But they only stared and laughed; and we walked unmolested to Mr. A___'s house.

I was quite surprised at the miserable condition of the fortifications; far more ruinous and decayed than those at Newcastle, even before the rebellion. It is well there is no enemy near.

I went to prayers at three in the old church, — a grand and venerable structure. Between five and six the coach called, and took me to Mighton-Car, about half a mile from the town. A huge multitude, rich and poor, horse and foot, with several coaches were soon gathered together...

GRIMSBY   BOSTON

GRIMSBY

Some thousands of the people seriously attended; but many behaved as if possessed by Moloch. Clods and stones flew about on every side; but they neither touched nor disturbed me. When I had finished my discourse, I went to take coach; but the coachman had driven clear away. We were at a loss, till a gentlewoman invited my wife and me to come into her coach. She brought some inconveniences on herself thereby; not only as there were nine of us in the coach, three on each side, and three in the middle; but also as the mob closely attended us, throwing in at the windows (which we did not think it prudent to shut) whatever came next to hand. But a large gentlewoman who sat in my lap screened me, so that nothing came near me.

1766 Friday, April 18 — I set out for the eastern part of Lincolnshire, and

after preaching at Awkborough and Barrow in the way, came the next day to our old friends at Grimsby. It put me in mind of Purrysburg, in Georgia. It was one of the largest towns in the county; it is no bigger than a middling village, containing a small number of half-starved inhabitants, without any trade, either foreign or domestic. But this they have; they love the Gospel, hardly six families excepted.

BOSTON CHURCH

1780 Friday, June 16 — We went on to Boston, the largest town in the county, except Lincoln. From the top of the steeple (which I suppose is by far the highest tower in the kingdom) we had a view not only of all the town, but of all the adjacent

LINCOLN

ARM OF THE CITY AND
SEE OF LINCOLN

country. Formerly this town was in the fens; but the fens are vanished away: great part of them is turned into pasture, and part into arable land. At six the house contained the congregation, all of whom behaved in the most decent manner. How different from those wild beasts with whom Mr. Mitchell and Mr. Mather had to do!

1782 Friday, May 10 —
I preached... in the evening at Epworth. I found the accounts I had received of the work of God here, were not at all exaggerated. Here is a little country town, containing a little more than eight or nine hundred grown people; and there has been such a work among them, as we have not seen in so short a time either at Leeds, Bristol or London.

Tuesday, May 14 — Some years ago four factories for spinning and weaving were set up at Epworth. In these a large number of young women, and boys and girls, were employed. The whole conversation of these was profane and loose to the last degree. But some of these stumbling in at the prayer-meeting were suddenly cut to the heart. These never rested till they had gained their companions. The whole scene was changed. In three of the factories, no more lewdness or profaneness were found; for God had put a new song in their mouth, and blasphemies were turned to praise.

THE MINSTER:
LINCOLN CATHEDRAL FROM THE SOUTH WEST

1790 Thursday, July 1 — I went to Lincoln. After
dinner we took a walk in and round the Minster; which I really think is more elegant than that at York, in various parts of the structure, as well as in its admirable situation. The new house was thoroughly filled in the evening, and with hearers uncommonly serious. There seems to be a remarkable difference between the people of Lincoln and those of York. They have not so much fire and vigour of spirit; but far more mildness and gentleness; by means of which, if they had the same outward helps, they would probably excel their neighbours.

THE DOCKS AT HULL

WILLIAM MASON THE POET, AND WILLIAM WILBERFORCE THE PHILANTHROPIST WERE BOTH 18TH CENTURY SONS OF THIS EAST RIDING SEAPORT

MANCHESTER

MANCHESTER (earlier named Mancunium by the Romans) may have seen the birth of Arkwright's spinning jenny and of Stephenson's railway engine 'Rocket', but its origin goes back to an era shrouded by fable and ballad. In the days of good King Arthur, Sir Launcelot of the Lake was said to be the hero in the downfall of a local giant:

Near Manchester there lived a knight of fame,
Of a prodigious strength and might,
Who vanquished many a worthy knight,
A giant great, and Tarquin was his name.

Certainly Manchester boasted a 'lang pedigree'. During the construction of the Bridgewater Canal, excavated Roman coins were those of Vespasian, Antoninus Pius, Trajan, Hadrian, Nero, Domitian, Vitellius and Constantine.

Change and controversy have often been a feature of Manchester. It suffered greatly from the Danish invasions, it saw the rapid growth of the textile industry, and it was often the centre of political turmoil. It was the English poet John Byrom (1692-1763), himself of Manchester, who wrote these amusing lines:

God bless the King, I mean our faith's defender;
God bless (no harm in blessing) the Pretender;
But who Pretender is – or who is King –
God bless us all – that's quite another thing.

Manchester, famous for its Cathedral, its university, its 'Guardian' newspaper and its Hallé orchestra, became a city in 1853.

SIR RICHARD ARKWRIGHT (1732 - 1792) INVENTOR OF THE SPINNING JENNY

1738

Tuesday, March 14 — I set out for Manchester, with Mr. Kinchin, Fellow of Corpus Christi, and Mr. Fox, late a prisoner in the city prison. About eight, it being rainy and very dark, we lost our way; but before nine, we came to Shipston, having rode over, I know not how, a narrow foot-bridge, which lay across a deep ditch near the town. After supper I read prayers to the people of the inn, and explained the Second Lesson; I hope not in vain.

ARMS OF THE CITY OF MANCHESTER

Thursday, March 16 — Late at night we reached Manchester. Friday, the 17th, we spent entirely with Mr. Clayton, by whom, and the rest of our friends here, we were much refreshed and strengthened. Mr. Hoole, the Rector of St. Ann's church, being taken ill the next day, on Sunday, the 19th, Mr. Kinchin and I officiated at Salford chapel in the morning, by which means Mr. Clayton was at liberty to perform the service of

PEEL PARK

St. Ann's; and in the afternoon I preached there on those words of St. Paul: "If any man be in Christ, he is a new creature." Early in the morning we left Manchester, taking with us Mr. Kinchin's brother, for whom we came, to be entered at Oxford.

1753 Saturday, March 31 — I preached at Boothbank, where I met Mr. C—, late gardener to the Earl of W—. Surely it cannot be! Is it possible the Earl should turn off an honest, diligent, well-tried servant, who had been in the family above fifty years, for no other fault than hearing the Methodists? In the evening I preached at Manchester; and on Monday, April 2, at Davyhulme. Here I found (what I had never heard of in England) a whole clan of infidel peasants. A neighbouring alehouse-keeper drinks, and laughs, and argues into Deism all the ploughmen and dairymen he can light on. But no mob raises against him; and reason good: Satan is not divided against himself.

Wednesday, April 4 — I made an end of examining the society at Manchester; among whom were seventeen of the Dragoons. It is remarkable, that these were in the same regiment with John Haime, in Flanders; but they utterly despised both him and his Master till they removed

THE ROYAL EXCHANGE, MANCHESTER

to Manchester: here it was that one and another dropped in, he scarce knew why, to hear the preaching. And they are now a pattern of seriousness, zeal and all holy conversation.

1755 Wednesday, April 9 — In the evening I preached at Manchester. The mob was tolerably quiet, as long as I was speaking, but immediately after, raged horribly. This, I find, has been their manner for some time. No wonder; since the good Justices encourage them.

STEPHENSON'S ROCKET MADE ITS APPEARANCE IN THE 19TH CENTURY

OWENS COLLEGE

1781 After preaching at Congleton, Macclesfield, and Stockport, in my way, on <u>Friday, March 30</u>, I opened the new chapel at Manchester, about the size of that in London. The whole congregation behaved with the utmost seriousness. I trust much good will be done in this place.

<u>Sunday, April 1</u> – I began reading prayers at ten o'clock. Our country friends flocked in from all sides. At the Communion was such a sight as I am persuaded was never seen at Manchester before: eleven or twelve hundred communicants at once; and all of them fearing God.

1776 <u>Thursday, April 4</u> – I began an answer to that dangerous Tract, Dr. Price's "Observations upon Liberty"; which if practised, would overturn all government, and bring in universal anarchy. On Easter-day the preaching house at Manchester contained the congregation pretty well at seven in the morning; but in the afternoon I was obliged to be abroad, thousands upon thousands flocking together. I stood in a convenient place, almost over against the infirmary, and exhorted a listening multitude to "live unto Him Who died for them and rose again."

"I trust much good will be done in this place."

Journals
March 30, 1781

OLDHAM STREET CHAPEL

MANCHESTER: 'THE FAIREST, BEST-BUILDED, QUICKLIEST AND MOST POPULOUS TOWNE OF AL LANCESTRESHIRE' (ANTIQUARY JOHN LELAND)
THE FREE TRADE HALL WAS BUILT IN THE 19TH CENTURY

BRISTOL

BRISTOL (Brigstow, Bristou, Bristow, Bristole) is an outstanding example of a town that has owed its prominence entirely to trade. It was the western limit of the Saxon invasion of Britain, and about the year 1,000 a Saxon settlement began to grow at the junction of the Rivers Frome and Avon.

In the eighteenth century Bristol became the centre of the Wesleyan revival. The city was cramped, densely populated and dirty, with dark narrow streets and no sanitary system. The mob gained an unenviable notoriety for its violence in the riots of 1708, 1753 and 1767.

The town's prosperity increased greatly during the eighteenth century, owing to the inhuman slave trade – the two or three thousand tons of shipping leaving England for Africa in 1714 was to rise to over fifteen thousand tons by the early sixties. Indeed England's growing maritime and colonial strength of that time is illustrated in the resolve of her merchants to initiate hostilities with Spain in 1739 – the very year when Wesley began to preach to the masses in the open air.

The Old Room in the Horsefair

MARYLEPORT STREET, BRISTOL

1739 Saturday, March 31 –

IN PITHAY, BRISTOL

In the evening I reached Bristol, and met Mr. Whitefield there. I could scarcely reconcile myself at first to this strange way of preaching in the fields, of which he set me an example on Sunday: having been all my life (till very lately) so tenacious of every point relating to decency and order, that I should have thought the saving of souls almost a sin, if it had not been done in a church.

Monday, April 2 – At four in the afternoon, I submitted to be more vile, and proclaimed in the highways the glad tidings of salvation, speaking from a little eminence in a ground adjoining to the city, to about three thousand people.

At seven I began expounding the Acts of the Apostles, to a society meeting in Baldwin-Street; and the next day the Gospel of St. John in the chapel at Newgate; where I also read the Morning Service of the Church.

Sunday, April 8 — At seven in the morning I preached to about a thousand persons at Bristol, and afterwards to about fifteen hundred on the top of Hannam Mount, in Kingswood. I called to them in the words of the evangelical prophet: "Ho! everyone that thirsteth, come ye to the waters; come and buy wine and milk, without money, and without price." About fifteen thousand were in the afternoon at Rose-Green (on the other side of Kingswood); among whom I stood and cried in the name of the Lord: "If any man thirst, let him come unto Me and drink. He that believeth on Me, as the Scripture hath said, out of his belly shall flow rivers of living water."

OUTDOOR PREACHING

1776 Monday, September 9 — I began, what I had long intended, visiting the society from house to house, setting apart at least two hours in a day for that purpose. I was surprised to find the simplicity with which one and all spoke, both of their temporal and spiritual state. Nor could I easily have known, by any other means, how great a work God has wrought among them. I found exceedingly little to reprove; but much to praise God for. And I observed one thing which I did not expect:— In visiting all the families, without Lawford-gate, by far the poorest about the city, I did not find so much as one person who was out of work.

Another circumstance I critically inquired into, What is the real number of the people?

The houses without Lawford-gate are computed to be a thousand. Now at the sitting of the Justices, some years since, there were two hundred public houses. Was then one house in five a public-house? No surely; one house in ten at the utmost. If so, there were two thousand houses; and consequently, fourteen thousand people.

1777 Monday, February 3 — Hearing there was some disturbance at Bristol, occasioned by men whose tongues were set on fire against the government, I went down in the diligence, and on Tuesday evening strongly enforced those solemn words: "Put them in mind to be subject to principalities and powers, to speak evil of no man." I believe God applied His Word, and convinced many that they had been out of their way.

Tuesday, December 16 — I paid a short visit to Bristol; preached in the evening and morning following, Wednesday 17 . . . Just at this time there was a combination among many of the post-chaise drivers on the Bath road, especially those that drove in the night, to deliver their passengers into each other's hands. One driver

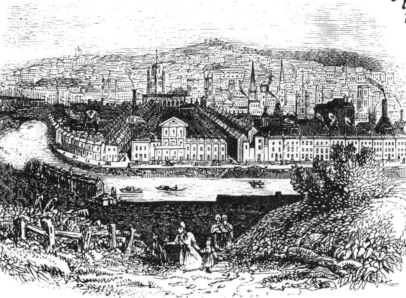

BRISTOL IN THE 17TH CENTURY

stopped at the spot they had appointed, where another waited to attack the chaise. In consequence of this, many were robbed; but I had a good protector still. I have travelled all roads, by day and by night, for these forty years, and never was interrupted yet.

1778 Tuesday, February 17 — I wrote "A Serious Address to the Inhabitants of England," with regard to the present state of the nation, — so strangely misrepresented both

by ignorant and designing men, — to remove, if possible, the apprehensions which have been so diligently spread, as if it were on the brink of ruin. Friday, 27, was the day appointed for the national fast; and it was observed with due solemnity. All shops were shut up; all was quiet in the streets; all places of public worship were crowded; no food was served in the the King's house till five o'clock in the evening. Thus far, at least, we acknowledge God may direct our paths.

1779 Wednesday, September 1 — A gentleman, just come from Plymouth, gave us a very remarkable account: — "For two days the combined fleets of France and Spain lay at the mouth of the harbour. They might have entered it with perfect ease. The wind was fair; there was no fleet to oppose them."
Why then did they not go in, destroy the dock, and burn, or at least plunder the town? I believe they could hardly tell themselves. — The plain reason was, the bridle of God

BRISTOL, FROM ST. AUGUSTINE'S QUAY

CLIFTON SUSPENSION BRIDGE
IN 1735 ALDERMAN VICK LEFT £1,000 FOR ITS ERECTION. WORK WAS NOT BEGUN TILL A CENTURY LATER.

was in their teeth; and He had said; "Hitherto shall ye come and no farther."

children showing that they were now managed with the wisdom that cometh from above.

1782 Friday, March 15 — In the evening I preached at Kingswood School, and afterwards met the bands. The colliers spoke without any reserve. I was greatly surprised: not only the matter of what they spoke was rational and Scriptural, but the language, yea, and the manner, were exactly proper. Who teacheth like Him?

1786 Friday, July 21 — I walked over to Kingswood-School, now one of the pleasantest spots in England. I found all things just according to my desire; the rules being well observed, and the whole behaviour of the

"The hospitality of the city was widely renowned"

— Macaulay, 'History of England'

PORTLAND SQUARE, BRISTOL

WEST RIDING of YORKSHIRE

BONNIE PRINCE CHARLIE

IT WAS IN 1742 that John Wesley visited Yorkshire for the first time. In what state did he find England's largest county? Some twenty years earlier Daniel Defoe had found it a rough ride as he travelled along the track from Lancashire into Yorkshire along the old Roman road over Blackstone Edge. The roads were terrible, the terrain threatening. Nevertheless, as he entered the towns and villages, he was able to report: 'Those people are full of business; not a beggar, not an idle person to be seen ... This business is the Clothing Trade ...' The beginning of the eighteenth century saw the Yorkshire worsted industry really flourishing, Halifax being its centre. 1733 was to see the invention of Kay's flying shuttle. The age was rough and brutal, and the Wesleys were to experience the full fury of the mobs that faced such sturdy Yorkshire preachers as William Grimshaw of Haworth, 'the Apostle of the North.'

Yorkshire's West Riding has become world-renowned for its beautiful dales, its superb architecture (Fountains Abbey being the finest of England's ruined abbeys) and its romantic history. Visitors by the thousand come to Haworth, which saw Wesley on seventeen separate occasions, and which boasted the Bröntes as its most celebrated family.

Wesley's journals make frequent reference to the political upheavals of his time. 'Bonnie Prince Charlie' (1720-1788) – the grandson of James II, and Pretender to the throne – was to rally a Highland army in the summer of 1745, and march into England in what proved to be the unsuccessful 'Jacobite' attempt to put the Stuarts on the throne. It was on November 5th of that year that Wesley arrived in Leeds.

1745

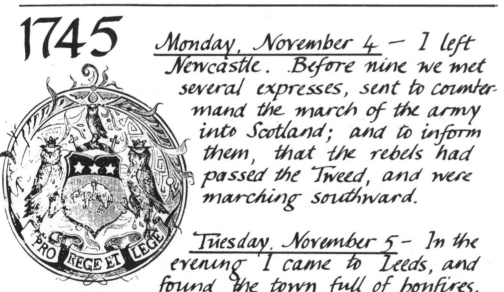

Monday, November 4 – I left Newcastle. Before nine we met several expresses, sent to countermand the march of the army into Scotland; and to inform them, that the rebels had passed the Tweed, and were marching southward.

Tuesday, November 5 – In the evening I came to Leeds, and found the town full of bonfires, and people shouting, firing of guns, cursing and swearing, as the English manner of keeping holidays is. I immediately sent word to some of the magistrates, of what I had heard

LEEDS, IN THE TIME OF JOHN WESLEY

LEEDS TODMORDEN

on the road. This ran through the town, as it were, in an instant: and I hope it was a token for good. The hurry in the streets was quashed at once; some of the bonfires indeed remained; but scarce anyone was to be seen about them, but a few children warming their hands.

1745 Friday, November 8 – Understanding that a neighbouring gentleman, Dr. C.,

THE MARKET PLACE, HUDDERSFIELD

had affirmed to many, that Mr. Wesley was now with the Pretender, near Edinburgh, I wrote him a few lines. It may be, he will have a little more regard to truth, or shame, for the time to come.

1746 Saturday, February 22 – (Leeds) – I preached at five. As we went home a great mob followed, and threw whatever came to hand. I was struck several times, once or twice in the face, but not hurt at all: I walked on to the Recorder's, and told him the case. He promised to prevent the like for the time to come.

1755 Friday, April 25 – About ten I preached near Todmorden. The people stood, row above row, on the side of the mountain. They were rough enough in outward appearance; but their hearts were as melting wax.

One can hardly conceive any

SURPRISE VIEW, FOUNTAINS ABBEY

thing more delightful than the vale through which we rode from thence. The river ran through the green meadows on the right. The fruitful hills and woods rose on either hand: yet here and there a rock hung over, the little holes of which put me in mind of those beautiful lines, –

Te, Domine, intonsi montes, te
     saxa loquentur
Summa Deum, dum montis amat
          juga pendulus hircus,
Saxorumque colit latebrosa
          cuniculus antra! *

* Paraphrase of Psalm 104 : "The high hills are a refuge for the wild goats and so are the stony rocks for the conies."

HUDDERSFIELD

1757 <u>Monday, May 9</u> – I rode over the mountains to Huddersfield. A wilder people I never saw in England. The men, women, and children filled the street as we rode along, and appeared just ready to devour us. They were, however, tolerably quiet while I preached; only a few pieces of dirt were thrown, and the bell-man came in the middle of the sermon, but was stopped by a gentleman of the town. I had almost done, when they began to ring the bells; so that it did us small disservice.

HAWORTH CHURCH AND REV. WILLIAM GRIMSHAW

HAWORTH

<u>Sunday, May 22</u> – After preaching at five, I took horse for Haworth. A December storm wet us upon the mountain; but this did not hinder such a congregation as the Church could not contain. I suppose we had nearly a thousand communicants, and scarcely a trifler among them.

1759 <u>Saturday, July 21</u> – Mr. Grimshaw led us to Gawksham, another lone house on the side of an enormous mountain. The congregation stood and sat, row above row, in the sylvan theatre. I believe nothing on the post-diluvian earth can be more pleasant than the road from hence, between huge, steep mountains, clothed with wood to the top, and washed at the

IN STUDLEY PARK

BINGLEY OTLEY BRADFORD

LABOR OMNIA VINCIT
ARMS OF BRADFORD

bottom by a clear, winding stream. At four I preached to a very large congregation at Heptonstall, and thence rode on to Haworth.

Sunday, July 22 — At ten, Mr. Milner read prayers; but the church would not near contain the congregation; so after prayers, I stood on a scaffold close to the church, and the congregation in the churchyard. The communicants alone filled the church. In the afternoon the congregation was nearly doubled; and yet most of these were not curious hearers, but men fearing God.

1766 Monday, August 4 — At one I preached at Bingley. In the afternoon I went to Otley; but the town seemed to be run mad. Such noise, hurry, drunkenness, rioting, confusion, I know not when I have met with before. It was their feast day! A feast of Bacchus, or Venus, or Belial? O shame to a Christian country!

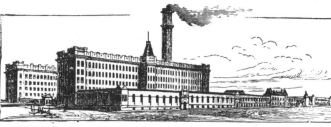

LISTER'S MILL, MANNINGHAM, NEAR BRADFORD

1775 Friday, August 4 — I preached at Bradford, where the people are all alive. Many here have lately experienced the great salvation, and their zeal has been a general blessing. Indeed, this I always observe, — wherever a work of sanctification breaks out, the whole work of God prospers. Some are convinced of sin, others justified, and all stirred up to greater earnestness for salvation.

1776 Sunday, April 28 — The congregation at Haworth was far greater than the church could contain. For the sake of the poor parishioners, few of whom are even awakened to this day, I spoke as strongly

as I possibly could upon these words: "The harvest is passed, the summer is ended, and we are not saved."

Monday, April 29 — About two I preached at Padiham, in a broad street to a huge congregation. I think the only inattentive persons were the minister and a kind of gentleman. I saw none inattentive at Clough in the evening. What has God wrought, since Mr. Grimshaw and I were seized near this place by a furious mob, and kept prisoners for some hours! The sons

MILL-HANDS AT SALTAIRE

PADIHAM   COLNE

of him who headed that mob now gladly receive our saying.

Tuesday, April 30 — In the evening I preached in a kind of square, at Colne, to a multitude of people, all drinking in the Word. I scarce ever saw a congregation wherein men, women and children stood in such a posture: and this in the town wherein, thirty years ago, no Methodist could show his head! The first that preached here was John Jane, who was innocently riding through the town, when the zealous mob pulled him off his horse, and put him in the stocks. He seized the opportunity, and vehemently exhorted them "to flee from the wrath to come."

DR. SMOLLETT

JOHN JANE PREACHING IN THE STOCKS

1779 Thursday, April 22 — I was a little surprised at a passage in Dr. Smollett's

"History of England," vol. xv., pp. 121, 122 :— "Imposture and fanaticism still hang upon the skirts of religion. Weak minds were seduced by the delusions of a superstition, styled Methodism, raised upon the affectation of superior sanctity, and pretensions to divine illumination. Many thousands were infected with this enthusiasm by the endeavours of a few obscure preachers, such as Whitefield, and the two Wesleys, who found means to lay the whole kingdom under contribution."

Poor Dr. Smollett! Thus to transmit to all succeeding generations a whole heap of notorious falsehoods! Meantime, what faith can be given to his History? What credit can any man of reason give to any fact upon his authority?

WAKEFIELD   HEPTONSTALL

1779 Wednesday, April 28 – I preached at Wakefield in the evening; Thursday, 29, at Rothwell and Leeds; and on Friday, noon, at Harewood. In the afternoon we walked to Mr. Lascelle's house. It is finely situated on a little eminence, commanding a most delightful prospect of hill and dale, and wood and water. It is built of fine white stone, with two grand and beautiful fronts. I was not struck with anything within. There is too much sameness in all the great houses I have seen in England, two rows of large, square rooms, with costly beds, glasses, chairs and tables. But here is a profusion of wealth; every pane of glass, we were informed, cost six-and-twenty shillings, one looking glass cost five hundred pounds, and one bed, six hundred. The whole floor was just on the plan of Montague-house; now the British Museum. The grounds round the house are pleasant indeed, particularly the walks on the river-side, and through the woods. But what has the owner thereof, save the beholding of them with his eyes?

HEPTONSTALL CHURCH

1780 Wednesday, April 19 – I went to Otley; but Mr. Ritchie was dead before I came. But he had first witnessed a good confession. One telling him, "You will be better soon;" he replied, "I cannot be better; for I have God in my heart. I am happy, happy, happy in His love!"

Mr. Wilson, the vicar, after a little hesitation, consented that I should preach his funeral sermon: this I did today. The text he had chosen was: "To you that believe, He is precious." Perhaps such a congregation had hardly been in Otley church before. Surely the right hand of the Lord bringeth mighty things to pass!

After preaching at several other places on Monday and Tuesday, Wednesday, 26, I preached in Heptonstall church, well filled with serious hearers.

In the evening I preached near Todmorden, in the heart of the mountains. One would wonder where all the people came from.

THE SEE OF WINCHESTER

ARMS OF THE CITY AND SEE OF WINCHESTER

RUFUS' STIRRUP

1 NEXTRICABLY LINKED with the ancient city and see of Winchester (Winton, Wynton) are the romantic figures of King Arthur and his knights; but it is to the late seventh century and to Hedda, first bishop of Winchester (d. 705), that we must go for our earliest reliable milestone. Winchester's position at the centre of six Roman roads indicates its early importance and indeed it was the seat of King Canute's government, rivalling, for a while, London itself as the capital of England. It gained its educational status through Alfred, and its great public school was originated in 1387 by the famous William of Wykeham. Its cathedral dates from Norman times, the magnificent perpendicular nave representing the later work of Bishop Edington (1346-1366) and William of Wykeham (1367-1404). Numerous tombs feature there, including that of the controversial Cardinal Beaufort.

The New Forest, in south-west Hampshire, was a hunting ground for the West Saxon kings, and is one of five forests mentioned in Domesday. William the Conqueror made it a royal forest; his two sons met their deaths within its boundaries – Richard being killed by a stag, and William Rufus by an arrow. Rufus' stone, near Lyndhurst, eventually marked the spot where the king was said to have fallen. The large stirrup that hung in the hall of Lyndhurst's 'Queen's House' (erected in Charles II's reign) has had only a legendary connection with Rufus.

1771 Thursday, October 3 – Winchester. I now found time to take a view of the cathedral. Here the sight of that bad Cardinal's tomb, whom the sculptor has placed in a position of prayer, brought to my mind those fine lines of Shakespeare, which he put into the mouth of King Henry the Sixth: —
"Lord Cardinal,
If thou hast any hope of Heaven's grace,
Give us a sign. He dies and makes no sign."

1781 Tuesday, October 9 – I preached at Winchester, where I went with great expectation to see that celebrated painting in the cathedral, the raising of Lazarus. But I was disappointed. I observed, 1. There was such a huddle of figures, that, had I not been told, I

GENERAL VIEW OF WINCHESTER

should never have guessed what they meant. 2. The colours in general were far too glaring, such as neither Christ nor His followers ever wore. When will painters have common sense?

Wednesday, October 10 – I opened the new preaching-house just finished at Newport, in the Isle of Wight. After preaching, I explained the nature of a Methodist society; of which few had before the least conception.

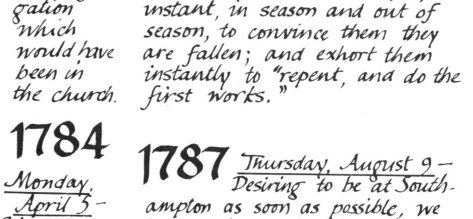

THE HIGH STREET, WINCHESTER

1783 Friday, October 10 – I crossed over to Southampton; and found two or three there also who feared and loved God. Then I went to Winchester. A clergyman having offered me his church, I purposed beginning at five; but the key was not to be found; so I made a virtue of necessity, and preached near the Cross-street; probably to double the congregation which would have been in the church.

WESTGATE, WINCHESTER

to the next generation! In the name of God, let us, if possible, secure the present generation from drawing back to perdition! Let all the preachers that are still alive to God join together as one man, fast and pray, lift up their voice as a trumpet, be instant, in season and out of season, to convince them they are fallen; and exhort them instantly to "repent, and do the first works."

1784 Monday, April 5 – We are labouring to secure the preaching-houses

1787 Thursday, August 9 – Desiring to be at Southampton as soon as possible, we took chaise at four in the morning, and (making but a short stay at Romsey) came thither between eight and nine. We found two

HIGH STREET, SOUTHAMPTON
ISAAC WATTS THE HYMN-WRITER WAS A PRODUCT (1674 — 1748) OF THIS ANCIENT SEAPORT

BAR GATE, SOUTHAMPTON

sloops nearly ready to sail. The captain of one promised to sail the next morning; so we sat down content. At seven in the evening I preached in Mr. Fay's school-room.

Saturday, 11 — We went on board The Queen, a small sloop, and sailed eight or nine leagues with a tolerable wind. But then it grew foul, and blew a storm; so that we were all glad to put in at Yarmouth harbour.

Monday, 13 — We set out from Yarmouth with a fair wind; but it soon turned against us and blew so hard that in the afternoon we were glad to put in at Swanage. I found we had still a little society here. I had not seen them for thirteen years, and had no thought of seeing them now; but God does all things well. In the evening I preached.

1790 Thursday, September 30 — It being a lovely morning, we went in a wherry, through Cowes harbour, to Newport; one of the pleasantest, neatest, and most elegant towns in the King's dominions.

" I abridged Dr. Watts' pretty 'Treatise on the Passions.' His hundred and seventy pages will make a useful tract of four- and - twenty."

Journals, 17th January, 1769

DR. WATTS

BROCKENHURST CHURCH

TRAVELS INTO SCOTLAND

ACROSS THE CENTURIES, Scotland (Caledonia) – the 'land of mountain and of flood' – has cherished a fiercely-defended independence. It has produced such fighting spirits as William Wallace and Robert Bruce, the leading figures in the wars of Scottish Independence. Charles Edward Stuart ('Bonnie Prince Charlie', 1720-1788) was causing a massive stir by his exploits at the very time of Wesley's ministry. Here is a land that has tested the bravest intruder by reason of its rocky coasts and its Southern Uplands; whose swift rivers and mighty heroes have evoked ballads and traditions in great profusion:

O roaring Clyde, ye roar ower loud,
Your streams seem wonder strang;
Mak me your prey as I come back,
But spare me as I gang.

Wesley visited Scotland a number of times, and found a religious climate that had been prepared by the earlier missionary endeavours of Ninian (c.400) and Columba (521-597). Later the sixteenth-century reformers such as Patrick Hamilton, George Wishart and – supremely – John Knox, had left a permanent mark upon Scottish Christianity. Here was the land of dissent, of the Kirk, and of the Bible.

1751

Wednesday, February 24 – Mr. Hopper and I took horse between three and four, and about seven came to Old-Camus. The Scotch towns are like none which I ever saw, either in England, Wales or Ireland: there is such an air of antiquity in them all, and such a peculiar oddness in their manner of building. But we were most surprised at the entertainment we met with in every place, so far different from common report. We had all things good, cheap, in great abundance, and remarkably well-dressed. In the afternoon we rode by Preston-field, and saw the place of battle, and Colonel Gardiner's house. The Scotch here affirm, that

JOHN KNOX
(c.1514 - 1572)

ON THE FORTH

PRINCES STREET, EDINBURGH

them seven or eight stories high,) is far beyond any in Great Britain. But how can it be suffered, that all manner of filth should still be thrown even into this street continually? Where are the magistracy, the gentry, the nobility of the land? Have they no concern for the honour of their nation? How long shall the capital city of Scotland, yea, and the chief street of it, stink worse than a common sewer? Will no lover of his country or of decency and common-sense find a remedy for this?

Holyrood-house, at the entrance of Edinburgh, the ancient palace of the Scottish Kings, is a noble structure. It was rebuilt and furnished by King Charles the Second. One side of it is a picture-gallery, wherein are pictures of all the Scottish Kings, and an original one of the celebrated Queen Mary: it is scarce possible for any who looks at this to think her such a monster as some have painted her; nor indeed for any who considers the circumstances of her death, equal to that of an ancient martyr.

HOLYROOD PALACE,
FOUNDED 1128, USED REGULARLY BY THE ROYAL FAMILY

1764 Thursday, June 7 — I rode over to Sir Archibald Grant's, twelve computed

he fought on foot after he was dismounted, and refused to take quarter. Be it as it may, he is now "where the wicked cease from troubling, and the weary are at rest."

LOCH CLARE & BEN LEAGACH

1761 Monday, May 11—(Edinburgh) The situation of the city, on a hill shelving down on both sides, as well as to the east, with the stately castle upon a craggy rock on the west, is inexpressibly fine. And the main street, so broad and finely paved, with the lofty houses on either hand (many of

BALMORAL CASTLE: GAELIC — 'THE MAJESTIC DWELLING'
THE PRIVATE RESIDENCE OF THE BRITISH SOVEREIGN SINCE 1852

KINGS COLLEGE, OLD ABERDEEN

Strathbogie, much improved by the linen-manufacture. All the country from Fochabers to Strathbogie has little houses scattered up and down; and not only the valleys, but the mountains themselves, are improved with the utmost care. There want only more trees to make them more pleasant than most of the mountains in England.

1774 Sunday, May 15 — (Glasgow). My spirit was moved within me at the sermons I heard both morning and afternoon. They contained much

miles from Aberdeen. It is surprising to see how the country between is improved even within these three years. On every side the wild, dreary moors are ploughed up, and covered with rising corn. All the ground near Sir Archibald's, in particular, is as well cultivated as most in England. About seven I preached. The kirk was pretty well filled, though upon short notice. Certainly this is a nation "swift to hear, and slow to speak," though not "slow to wrath."

Tuesday, June, 12 — We rode through the pleasant and fertile county of Murray to Elgin. At Elgin are the ruins of a noble cathedral; the largest that I remember to have seen in the kingdom. We rode thence to Spey, the most rapid river, next the Rhine, that I ever saw. Though the water was not breast-high to our horses, they could very hardly keep their feet. We dined at Keith, and rode on to

GLAMIS CASTLE

truth, but were no more likely to awaken one soul than an Italian opera. In the evening a multitude of people assembled on the green, to whom I earnestly applied these words: "Though I have all knowledge, – though I have all faith, – though I give all my goods to feed the poor," etc., "and have not love, I am nothing."

Saturday, 21 – I returned to Perth, and preached in the evening to a large congregation. But I could not find the way to their hearts. The generality of the people here are so wise that they need no more knowledge, and so good that they need no more religion! Who can warn them that are brimful of wisdom and goodness, to flee from the wrath to come?

1776 Monday, May 20 – Banff is one of the neatest and most elegant towns that I have seen in Scotland. It is pleasantly situated on the side of a hill, sloping from the sea, though close to it; so that it is sufficiently sheltered from the sharpest winds. The streets are straight and broad. I believe it may be esteemed the fifth, if not the fourth, town in the kingdom. The country quite from Banff to Keith is the best peopled of any I have seen in Scotland.

RUINS OF ST. ANDREW'S CATHEDRAL

Monday, 27 – I paid a visit to St. Andrews, once the largest city in the kingdom. It was eight times as large as it is now, and a place of very great trade; but the sea rushing from the north-east, gradually destroyed the harbour and trade together; in consequence of which, whole streets (that were) are now meadows and gardens. Three broad, straight handsome streets remain, all pointing at the old cathedral; which, by the ruins, appears to have been above three hundred feet long, and proportionately broad and high: so that it seems to have exceeded York Minster, and to have at least equalled any cathedral in England. Another church, afterwards used in its stead, bears date 1124. A steeple, standing near the cathedral, is thought to have stood thirteen hundred years.

1784 Saturday, May 1 – I went to Dundee, through the Carse of Gowry, the fruitfullest valley in the kingdom. And I observe a spirit of improvement prevails in Dundee, and all the country round about it. Handsome houses spring up on every side. Trees are planted in abundance. Wastes and commons are continually turned into meadows and fruitful fields. There wants only

1. ABERGELDIE CASTLE
2. CRATHIE PARISH CHURCH
3. BRAEMAR CASTLE

a proportionable improvement in religion, and this will be one of the happiest countries in Europe.

Friday, May 7 – (Fort-Glen). I took a walk round about the town. I know not when I have seen so pleasant a place. One part of the house is an ancient castle, situated on the top of a little hill. At a small distance runs a clear river, with a beautiful wood on its banks. Close to it is a shady walk to the right, and another on the left hand. On two sides of the house there is abundance of wood; on the other, a wide prospect over fields and meadows. About ten I preached again with much liberty of spirit, on: "Love never faileth."

"The Scotch towns are like none which I ever saw . . ."

Journals, February 24, 1751

"LET GLASGOW FLOURISH BY THE PREACHING OF THE WORD" — THE TRADITIONAL CITY MOTTO
(THE BROOMIELAW BRIDGE WAS FIRST USED IN 1835; RECONSTRUCTED 1899)

LIVERPOOL AND MERSEY-

THE PERCH ROCK LIGHTHOUSE

LIVERPOOL, the centre of Merseyside, may have derived its name from the Norse *Hlithar-pollr*, 'the pool of the slopes', colonies of Norsemen having settled on both sides of the Mersey in the eighth century. A favourite explanation, however, is that the name is taken from the heraldic bird, the 'Liver' – a bird of no known species, but said to be of aquatic habits. Certainly there was a bird upon Liverpool's corporation seal at least as far back as the reign of King John.

Liverpool's growth only came about slowly, being little more than a fishing village at the time of William the Conqueror, and suffering from such adversities as the Black Death in 1360, and the Civil War – in which it sustained three sieges. A census at the end of the thirteenth century gave its population as 800, and its number of houses 168. It was the rise of South Lancashire's industry and the opening of trade with America and the West Indies that was to transform Liverpool into a major city of commerce, at the beginning of the eighteenth century. Throughout the century Liverpool was the centre of the English slave trade, which was finally abolished in 1807. The American War of Independence (1775) gravely threatened the livelihood of the Liverpool slave traders, Wesley making mention of this in his journals.

MERSEYSIDERS BOARDING SHIP

1755 Tuesday, April 15 – Warrington: at six in the morning, I preached to a large and serious congregation; and then

LIVERPOOL ABOUT 1755

went on to Liverpool, one of the neatest, best-built towns I have seen in England: I think it is fully twice as large as Chester; most of the streets are quite straight. Two thirds of the town, we were informed, have been added within these forty years. If it continue to increase in the same proportion, in forty years more it will nearly equal Bristol. The people in general are the most mild and corteous I ever saw in a sea-port town; as indeed appears by their friendly behaviour, not only to the Jews and Papists who live among them, but even to the Methodists (so called). The preaching-house is a little larger than that at Newcastle. It was thoroughly filled at seven in the evening; and the hearts of the whole congregation seemed to be moved before the Lord, and before the presence of His power. Every morning, as well as evening,

LIVERPOOL PORT: HOME OF MERSEYSIDERS SINCE THE EIGHTH CENTURY NORSEMEN

CORNWALL - ITS FISHING

ROCKS AT KYNANCE

THE INFLUENCE OF THE WESLEYS upon Cornwall is in full evidence today, through the numerous Methodist chapels that confront the visitor to England's most westerly region – the last part of southern England to have fallen to the ninth-century Saxon invaders. The mobs that Wesley faced at St. Ives and Falmouth were as rugged in spirit as the rocky coastline at Land's End, where, legend has it, 'that last battle in the west' was fought by King Arthur.

Cornwall's aura of romance was perpetuated in such figures as Edward, 'the Black Prince', hero of Crecy and Poitiers, and one of the original Knights of the Garter, becoming Duke of Cornwall in 1337 – the first Duke ever created in England. It was the giant Cormoran whom tradition credits as erecting the first building on the legendary St. Michael's Mount – in its lifetime both a fortress and an ecclesiastical foundation. This mass of granite finds a place in Milton's 'Lycidas'.

CORNISH HEATH
(ERICA VAGANS)

The sea and underground mineral wealth – here for centuries lay the very life of Cornwall, celebrated for its fishing industry and its tin mines. It was to this captivating peninsula that the Wesleys came in 1743, and heard the ditty sung under their window at St. Ives:

Charles Wesley is come to town,
To try if he can pull the churches down.

1743 Friday, September 16 – As I was preaching at St. Ives, Satan began to fight for his kingdom. The mob of the town burst into the room, and created much disturbance; roaring and striking those that stood in their way, as though Legion himself possessed them. I would fain have persuaded our people to stand still; but the zeal of some, and the fear of others had no ears: so that, finding the uproar increase, I went into the midst, and brought the head of the mob up with me to the desk. I received but one blow on the side of the head; after which we reasoned the case, till he grew milder and milder, and at length undertook to quiet his companions.

LAND'S END

NEWLYN, WITH PENZANCE IN THE DISTANCE

VILLAGES, CHAPELS AND MINES

ST. MICHAEL'S MOUNT

Finding the justices were not met, we walked up St. Michael's Mount. The house at the top is surprisingly large and pleasant. Sir John St. Aubyn had taken much pains, and been at a considerable expense, in repairing and beautifying the apartments; and when the seat was finished, the owner died!

Tuesday, June 25 – We rode to St. Just. I preached at seven. When the preaching was ended,

1744 Thursday, April 4 – (St. Ives). I took a view of the ruins of the house which the mob had pulled down a little before, for joy that Admiral Matthews had beat the Spaniards. Such is the Cornish method of thanksgiving. I suppose, if Admiral Lestock had fought too, they would have knocked all the Methodists on the head.

1745 Friday, June 21 – We rode to Marazion. (Vulgarly called Market-jew.)

" WE RODE TO ST. JUST "

the constable apprehended Edward Greenfield, (by a warrant from Dr. Borlase,) a tinner, in the forty-sixth year of his age, having a wife and seven children. Three years ago he was eminent for cursing, swearing, drunkenness, and all manner of wickedness; but those old things had been for some time passed away, and he was then remarkable for a quite contrary behaviour.

I asked a little gentleman at St. Just, what objection there was to Edward Greenfield. He said, "Why, the man is well enough in other things; but his impudence the gentlemen cannot bear. Why, Sir, he says he knows his sins are forgiven!" And for this cause he is adjudged to banishment or death!

ROCKS NEAR THE LIZARD

Thursday, July 4 — I rode to Falmouth. About three in the afternoon I went to see a gentlewoman who had been long indisposed. Almost as soon as I was set down, the house was beset on all sides by an innumerable multitude of people. A louder or more confused noise could hardly be at the taking of a city by storm. The rabble roared with all their throats, "Bring out the Canorum! Where is the Canorum?" (An unmeaning word which the Cornish generally use instead of Methodist. Away went all the hinges at once, and the door fell back into the room. I stepped forward at once into the midst of them, and said, "Here I am. Which of you has anything to say to me? To which of you have I done any wrong? To you? Or you? Or you?" I continued speaking . . . and, as far as the sound reached, the people were

FALMOUTH: 'THE PRINCIPLE HAVEN OF ALL BRITAIN' (ANTIQUARY JOHN LELAND)

still; till one or two of their captains turned about and swore that not a man should touch him. Mr. Thomas, a clergyman, then came up and asked, "Are you not ashamed to use a stranger thus?" He was soon seconded by two or three gentlemen of the town, and one of the aldermen; with whom I walked down the town, speaking all the time, till I came to Mrs. Maddern's house.

1747 Tuesday, June 30 – We came to St. Ives before morning prayers, and walked to church without so much as one huzza. How strangely has one year changed the scene in Cornwall! This is now a peacable, nay, honourable station. They give us good words in almost every place. What have we done, that the world should be so civil to us?

1753 Tuesday, July 31 – (after illness). After living a day and a half on claret and water, I found myself so easy, that I thought I could ride to Crowan. I found no inconvenience the first hour; but in the second my disorder returned. However, I rode on, being unwilling to

JOHN WESLEY RIDING THROUGH CAMBORNE

disappoint the congregation, and preached on: "Be careful for nothing." I then rode straight, as fast as I conveniently could, to Mr. Harris's, in Camborne.

FISHING BOATS COMING HOME. IT IS THE PILCHARD WHICH FIGURES IN THE OLD CORNISH TOAST: "TIN, FISH AND COPPER"

1762 Sunday, September 5 – I could not stand in the usual place at Gwennap. But at a small distance was a hollow capable of containing many thousand people. I stood

WESLEY PREACHING IN GWENNAP PIT

Gwennap; far the finest I know in the kingdom. It is a round, green hollow, gently shelving down, about fifty feet deep; but I suppose it is two hundred across one way, and near three hundred the other.

1778 Monday, August 31 – About eleven I preached to a large and serious congregation, near the town-hall, in Bodmin; and about six in the evening at Launceston; a town as little troubled with religion as most in Cornwall.

on one side of this amphitheatre toward the top, with the people beneath and on all sides, and enlarged on those words in the Gospel for the day (Luke X. 23, 24): "Blessed are the eyes which see the things that ye see, and which hear the things that ye hear."

1781 Monday, August 27 – I was desired to preach at Trenuth at noon, a little way (they said) out of the road. The little way proved six or seven miles, through a road ready to break our wheels in pieces. However I just reached St. Austell in time enough to preach; and God greatly comforted the hearts of His people.

1766 Sunday, September 14 – I preached in St. Agnes at eight. The congregation in Redruth, at one, was the largest I ever had seen there; but small compared to that which assembled at five, in the natural amphitheatre at

POLPEOR

Tuesday, 28 – Between nine and ten we had such a storm of rain, as I do not remember to have seen in Europe before. It seemed ready to beat in the windows of the chaise, and in three minutes drenched our horsemen from head to foot. We reached Truro, however, at the appointed time . . .

In the evening I preached in the High-street at Helston. I scarce know a town in the whole country which is so totally changed; not a spark of that bitter enmity to the Methodists, in which the people here gloried above their fellows.

In the evening I preached the market-place at Penzance... This is another of the towns wherein the whole stream of the people is turned, as it were, from east to west.

1781 Saturday, September 1 – At eleven I preached in Camborne church-town; and I believe the hearts of all the people were bowed down before the Lord.

PENZANCE

'How strangely has one year changed the scene in Cornwall!'

Journals, June 30, 1747

DURHAM AND THE WEAR

THE FAMOUS SANCTUARY-KNOCKER
ON THE CATHEDRAL'S NORTH DOOR.

DURHAM (Dunholme, Dunelm, Duresme) is not as ancient a centre as its appearance and strategic position might suggest. There is no evidence of an early English settlement on the bold headland that was carved out by the River Wear, on its way from the Pennines to the North Sea. The earliest inhabitants of the site were the monks of Lindisfarne who, from fear of Danish invaders, had removed the body of St. Cuthbert (c. 634-687) from its tomb, and brought it to its new resting place in 999 – where it has stayed for nearly a thousand years.

The present cathedral was built in Norman times, and is unsurpassed by any other Norman church. It marks another resting place – that of 'the Venerable Bede' (c. 673-735), commonly acknowledged as 'the founder of medieval history, and the first English historian'. Durham Castle was built in 1072 by William the Conqueror, positioned to the north of the cathedral, across the neck of the peninsula. Durham University was not to receive its charter until 1837, from William IV, although a strong educational connection dates back to Prior Richard de Hoton and Bishop Hatfield, in the thirteenth and fourteenth centuries.

1772

Tuesday, June 2 – We rode to New-Orygan, in Teesdale. The people were deeply attentive; but, I think, not deeply affected. From the top of the next enormous mountain, we had a view of Weardale. It is a lovely prospect. The green gently-rising meadows and fields, on both sides of the little river, clear as crystal, were sprinkled over with innumerable little houses; three in four of which (if not nine in ten) are sprung up since the Methodists came hither. Since that time, the beasts are turned into men, and the wilderness into a fruitful field.

Thursday, 4 – At five I took my leave of this blessed people. I was a little surprised, in looking attentively upon them, to observe so many beautiful faces as I never saw before in

THE NAVE
DURHAM CATHEDRAL
THE CHOIR

one congregation; many of the children in particular, twelve or fourteen of whom (chiefly boys) sat full in my view. But I allow, much more

VALLEY

ARMS OF THE CITY AND
SEE OF DURHAM

might be owing to grace than nature, to the heaven within that shone outward.

In this part of Weardale, the people in general are employed in the lead-mines.

1774 Sunday, June 26 – In the morning I preached at the Ballast-hills, among the glassmen, keelmen, and sailors. As these had nothing to pay, I exhorted them "to buy wine and milk without money and without price."

Monday, 27 – I took my leave of this lovely place and people, and about ten preached to a serious congregation at Durham. About six I preached at Stockton-upon-Tees, on a text suited to the congregation: "Where their worm dieth not, and the fire is not quenched."

Tuesday, 28 – This being my birthday, the first day of my seventy-second year, I was considering, How is this, that I find just the same strength as I did thirty years ago? That my sight is considerably better now, and my nerves firmer, than they were then? That I have none of the infirmities of old age, and have lost several I had in my youth? The grand cause is, the good pleasure of God, Who doeth whatsoever pleaseth Him. The chief means are, 1. My constantly rising at four, for about

fifty years. 2. My generally preaching at five in the morning; one of the most healthy exercises in the world. 3. My never travelling less than four thousand five hundred miles in a year.

GENERAL VIEW OF THE CATHEDRAL AND CASTLE

1777 Monday, May 5 – Having finished my business in these parts (Sunderland), I set my face southward again; and after preaching at Durham, about eleven went on to Darlington. I have not lately found so lively a work in any part of England as here. The society is constantly increasing, and seems to be all on fire for God. There is nothing among them but humble, simple love; no dispute, no

NORMAN DOORWAY IN DURHAM CASTLE

jar of any kind. They exactly answer the description that David Brainerd gives of his Indian congregation.

1779 Wednesday, May 12—

After preaching at Cuthberton and in Teesdale, I went a little out of my way, to see one of the wonders of nature. The river Tees rushes down between two rocks, and falls sixty feet perpendicular into a basin of water, sixty feet deep. In the evening I preached to the lovely congregation in Weardale, and the next day went on to New-castle.

1780 Wednesday, May 31—

In the afternoon we took a view of the castle at Durham, the residence of the bishop. The situation is wonderfully fine, surrounded by the river, and commanding all the country; and many of the apartments are large and stately; but the furniture is mean beyond imagination! I know not where I have seen such in a gentleman's house, or a man of five hundred a year, except that of the Lord-Lieutenant in Dublin. In the largest chambers, the tapestry is quite faded; beside that, it is coarse and ill-judged. Take but one instance:— In Jacob's vision you see, on the one side, a little paltry ladder, and an angel climbing it, in the attitude of a chimney-sweeper; and on the other side Jacob staring at him, from under a large silver-laced hat!

THE TOMB OF BEDE,
DURHAM CATHEDRAL

Thursday, June 1 — About ten I preached at Aycliffe, a large village, twelve miles from Durham; all the inhabitants whereof seem now as full of good will, as they were once of prejudice.

1786 Saturday, June 10 —

I went to Darlington. Since I was here last, Mr. — died, and left many thousand

DURHAM FROM THE RIVER: 'THE SITE WAS CHOSEN TO DEFEND THE CORPSE RATHER THAN THE LIFE OF A MAN'

pounds to an idle spendthrift, but not one groat to the poor. O unwise steward of the mammon of unrighteousness! How much better for him had he died a beggar!

DURHAM CATHEDRAL FROM THE SOUTH-WEST

Durham:

"The situation is wonderfully fine; surrounded by the river and commanding all the country."

Journals, May 31, 1780

KENT - ENGLAND'S GATEWAY

THROUGHOUT early English history, Kent has been seen as the Gateway to England, and Dover Castle as the key. To this day the High Street in Rochester follows the line of the old Watling Street – the great Roman highway that led from the Kentish coast to London, and on to the north. Along this road the Roman legions marched; the English invaders followed, succeeded in turn by the missionaries of Gregory, and a host of kings, knights and pilgrims.

SHAKESPEARE'S CLIFF, DOVER

The diocese of Canterbury was founded in 597 with the arrival of Augustine, and that of Rochester in 600. The neighbourhood of Rochester and Chatham features prominently in the writings of Charles Dickens (1812-1870), Chatham having been his home in early childhood. Of Rochester (under the name of Cloisterham), he wrote: 'Its antiquities and ruins are surpassingly beautiful, with the lusty ivy gleaming in the sun, and the rich trees waving in the balmy air. Changes of glorious light from moving boughs, songs of birds, scents from gardens, woods and fields – or, rather, from the one great garden of the whole cultivated island in its yielding time – penetrate into the cathedral, subdue its earthy odour, and preach the Resurrection and the Life.' It was into Kent, 'The Garden of England', that John Wesley rode one Monday in November, at the age of forty-eight.

CHARLES DICKENS
MAN OF KENT

1751 Monday, November 11 – I rode to Rochester, and the next day to Canterbury, where I preached, morning and evening, in what was lately the French Church. We had not any disturbance from first to last, the Court of the King's Bench having broke the spirits of the rioters.

1756 Monday, October 11 – I went to Leigh. In this little journey, I read over a curiosity indeed, – a French heroic poem, Voltaire's "Henriade". He is a very lively writer, of a fine imagination; and allowed, I suppose, by all competent judges, to be a perfect master of the French language: and by him I was more than ever convinced that the French is the poorest, meanest language in Europe; that it is no more comparable to the German or Spanish than a bag-pipe is to an organ . . .

WEST GATE, CANTERBURY

1766 Wednesday, November 5 – I rode by Shoreham to Sevenoaks. In the little journeys which I have lately taken, I have thought much on the huge encomiums which have

take a detail of his happiness. He rises with, or before the sun, calls his servants, looks to his swine and cows, then to his stable and barns. He sees to the ploughing and sowing his ground, in winter or in spring. In summer and autumn he hurries and sweats among his mowers and reapers. And where is his happiness in the meantime? Which of these employments do we envy? Or do we envy the delicate repast that succeeds, which the poet so languishes for? — "O the happiness of eating beans well greased with fat bacon! Nay, and cabbage too!" — Was Horace in his senses when he talked thus, or the servile herd of his imitators? Our eyes and ears may convince us there is not a less happy body of men in all England than the country farmers. In general, their life is supremely dull; and it is usually unhappy too. For of all people in the kingdom, they are most discontented; seldom satisfied either with God or man.

ARMS OF THE CITY AND SEE OF CANTERBURY

"SEE THAT LITTLE HOUSE UNDER THE WOOD".

been for many ages bestowed on a country life. How have all the learned world cried out,
O fortunati nimium, sua
si bona norint,
Agricolae! *

But after all, what a flat contradiction is this to universal experience! See that little house, under the wood, by the river side! There is rural life in perfection. How happy then is the farmer that lives there! Let us

*"Too happy, if their happiness they knew!"

TUNBRIDGE WELLS, FROM MOUNT EPHRAIM

TONBRIDGE CASTLE, BUILT IN HENRY 1's REIGN, BESIEGED BY WILLIAM RUFUS, LATER CAPTURED BY JOHN AND EVENTUALLY DISMANTLED DURING THE CIVIL WAR.

1770

Wednesday, December 5 — We went to Dover, where with some difficulty we climbed to the top of Shakespeare's cliff. It is exceeding high, and commands a vast prospect both by sea and land; but it is nothing so terrible in itself as it is in his description.* I preached to a very serious congregation in the evening as well as in the morning.

CANTERBURY VIEWED FROM HARBLEDOWN

1772

Wednesday, December 2 — I preached at the new preaching-house, in the parish of Bromley. In speaking severally to the members of the society, I was surprised at the openness and artlessness of the people. Such I should never have expected to find within ten miles of London.

---

* "— whose high and bending head
Looks fearfully on the confined deep."

Friday, 11 — Passing through Sittingbourne, I found a congregation ready; so I gave them a short discourse, and went on to Chatham.

Monday, 14 — I read prayers and preached to a crowded congregation at Gravesend. The stream here spreads wide, but it is not deep. Many are drawn, but none converted, or even awakened. Such is the general method of God's

PENSHURST CHURCH

RUINS OF SISSINGHURST

1778 Monday, January 19 — I went over to Tunbridge Wells, and preached in the large Dissenting meeting, to a numerous congregation; and deep attention sat on every face.

Wednesday, November 4 — I took a view of the old church at Minster, once a spacious and elegant building. It stands pleasantly on the top of a hill, and commands all the country round. We went from thence to Queensborough, which contains above fifty houses, and sends two members to Parliament. Surely the whole Isle of Sheppey is now but a shadow of what it once was.

Thursday, 5 — I returned to Chatham, and on the following morning set out in the stage coach for London. At the end of Stroud, I chose to walk up the hill, leaving the coach to follow me. But it was in no great haste: it did not overtake me till I had walked about five miles. I cared not if it had been ten: the more I walk the sounder I sleep.

providence: where all approve, few profit.

1774 Monday, December 6 — I went to Canterbury in the stage-coach, and by the way read Lord Herbert's Life, written by himself; the author of the first system of Deism that ever was published in England. Was there ever so wild a knight-errant as this? Compared to him Don Quixote was a sober man.

SALUTING BATTERY GATE, DOVER CASTLE

PENSHURST PLACE, HOME OF SIR PHILIP SIDNEY (1554 — 1586)

1780 Tuesday, October 17 — I came back to Sevenoaks and in the afternoon walked over to the Duke of Dorset's seat. The park is the pleasantest I ever saw; the trees are so elegantly disposed. The house which is at least two hundred years old, is immensely large. The tapestry, representing the whole history of Nebuchadnezzar, is as fresh as if newly woven. But the bed-curtains are exceeding dirty, and look more like copper than gold. The silver on the tables, chair and glass, looks as dull as lead . . .

1781 Wednesday, November 28 — I preached at Tunbridge-Wells, in the large, Presbyterian meeting-house, to a well-dressed audience, and yet deeply serious. On Thursday I preached at Sevenoaks.

1785 Wednesday, November 30 — I went on to Margate. Some years since, we had a small society here; but a local-preacher took them to himself: only two or three remained, who, from time to time, pressed our preachers to come again; and, to remove the objection, that there was no place to preach in, with the help of a few friends they built a convenient preaching-house.

Thursday, December 1 — I opened it in the evening: the congregation was large, and perfectly well-behaved; and I cannot but hope, that, after all the stumbling blocks, there will be a people here, who will uniformly adorn the Gospel of Christ.

ROCHESTER CASTLE FROM THE MEDWAY

Bromley:
" I was surprised at the openness and artlessness of the people " —

Journals, December 2, 1772

BIRMINGHAM AND THE

ARMS OF THE CITY
OF BIRMINGHAM

IN THE MIDLANDS we come to the very heart and powerhouse of England, where intense industrial expansion was to develop throughout Wesley's itinerant ministry. Earlier the Midlands had set the stage for the two great battles that began and ended the Civil War (1642-1645) – Edgehill and Naseby; Warwickshire and Northamptonshire serving as busy crossroads for Parliamentarians and Royalists alike.

This is Shakespeare's country too, for the Avon rises quite near Naseby, flowing south-westerly to Rugby – where the famous public school is Thomas Arnold's greatest monument – and on through Warwick, and past Stratford-on-Avon itself. The Midlands threw up in Wesley's time a brilliant array of great names. John Fletcher, the godly rector of Madeley was marked out by Wesley as his successor – though this was not to be so. Josiah Wedgwood (1730-1795) became the world's greatest potter; William Murdock (1754-1839) was linked with the first manufacture of gas; and Birmingham may claim for herself the development of the steam engine through James Watt (1736-1819) and Matthew Boulton (1728-1809). Such change we contrast with John Leland's description of England's second city as recently as the sixteenth century: 'Bermingham, a good markett towne in the extreame parts of Warwickeshire, is one street going up alonge, almost from the left ripe of the brooke, up a meane hill by the length of a quarter of a mile. I saw but one parroch church in the towne.'

SWORDS FOUND
AT EDGEHILL, AND
BADGE OF CHARLES I

1743 Thursday, October 20 – I rode to Wednesbury.

At twelve I preached in a ground near the middle of town, to a far larger congregation than was expected, on: "Jesus Christ, the same yesterday, and today, and for ever." I believe everyone present felt the power of God.

I was writing at Francis Ward's, in the afternoon, when the cry arose, that the mob had beset the house. . . . The cry of one and all was, "Bring out the minister; we will have the minister." I desired one to take their captain by the hand, and bring him into the house. After a few sentences interchanged between us, the lion was become a lamb. I desired him to go and bring one or two more of the most angry of his companions. He brought in two, who were ready to swallow the ground with rage; but in two minutes

JOHN WESLEY AT WEDNESBURY

MIDLANDS

they were as calm as he. I then bade them make way, that I might go out among the people. As soon as I was in the midst of them, I called for a chair; and standing up, asked "What do any of you want with me?" Some said, "We want you to go with us to the Justice." I replied, "That I will, with all my heart." I then spoke a few words which God applied; so that they cried out, with might and main, "The gentleman is an honest gentleman, and we will spill our blood in his defence."

... A little before ten, God brought me safe to Wednesbury, having lost only one flap of my waistcoat, and a little skin from one of my hands.

MILL AT EDGEHILL

CHURCH AND VICARAGE, MADELEY, SHROPSHIRE

1764 Saturday, July 21 – I rode to Bilbrook, near Wolverhampton, and preached between two and three. Thence we went on to Madely an exceeding pleasant village, encompassed with trees and hills.

Sunday, 22 – At ten Mr. Fletcher read prayers, and I preached on those words in the Gospel: "I am the Good Shepherd: the good Shepherd layeth down His life for the sheep." The church would nothing near contain the congregation; but a window near the pulpit being taken down, those who could not come in stood in the churchyard, and I believe all could hear.

1778 Friday, March 20 – I preached at Birmingham.

Saturday, March 21 – Calling at Wolverhampton, I

was informed that, some time since, a large, old house was taken, three or four miles from the town, which receives all the children that come, sometimes above four hundred at once. They are taught, gratis, reading, writing and Popery; and, when of age, bound out apprentices.

1779 Wednesday, July 21 — When I came to Coventry, I found notice had been given for my preaching in the park; but the heavy rain prevented. I sent to the Mayor, desiring the use of the town-hall. He refused; but the same day gave the use of it to a dancing master. I then went to the women's market. Many soon gathered together, and listened with all seriousness. I preached there again the next morning, Thursday, 22, and again in the evening. Then I took coach for London. I was nobly attended: behind the

ST. MARTIN'S, BIRMINGHAM'S
'ONE PARROCH CHURCH', DESCRIBED BY LELAND, REBUILT SINCE HIS TIME

coach were ten convicted felons, loudly blaspheming and rattling their chains; by my side sat a man with a loaded blunderbuss and another upon the coach.

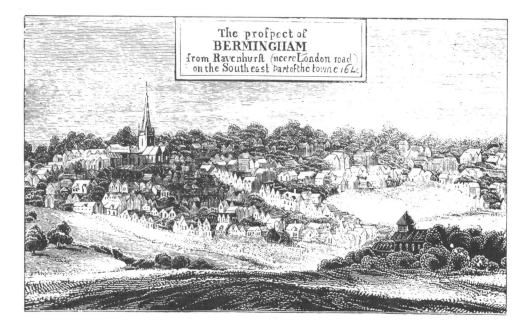

The prospect of
BERMINGHAM
from Ravenhurst (neere London road)
on the South east Part of the towne 1640

1782 Thursday, July 4 — I preached at Derby. I trust the work of God will now prosper here also.

Friday, 12 — (Birmingham) I walked through Mr. Bolton's curious works. He has carried every thing which he takes in hand to a high degree of perfection, and employs

BIRMINGHAM: HOME OF THE BOULTON AND WATT STEAM ENGINE

THE CHAPEL
EXTERIOR OF
RUGBY
SCHOOL
(FOUNDED
1567)
AND THOMAS
ARNOLD, ITS
MOST FAMOUS
HEADMASTER
(1827 - 1842)

I never was so surprised. I have seen nothing in all England to be compared with it. It is beautiful and elegant all over. There is nothing grand, nothing costly; no temples, so called; no statues; (except two or three, which had better have been spared;) but such walks, such shades, such hills and dales, such lawns, such artless cascades, such waving woods, with water intermixed, as exceed all imagination! On the upper side, from the openings of a shady walk, is a most beautiful and extensive prospect. And all this is comprised in the compass of three miles. I doubt if it be exceeded by any thing in Europe.

Sunday, 14 — I heard a sermon in the old church at Birmingham, which the preacher uttered with great vehemence against these "harebrained, itinerant enthusiasts." But he totally missed his mark; having not the least conception of the persons whom he undertook to describe.

in the house about five hundred men, women, and children. His gardens, running along the side of a hill, are delightful indeed; having a large piece of water at the bottom, in which are two well-wooded islands. If faith and love dwell here, then there may be happiness too. Otherwise all these beautiful things are as unsatisfactory as straws and feathers.

Saturday, 13 — I spent an hour in Hagley-park; I suppose inferior to few, if any, in England. But we were straitened for time. To take a proper view of it would require five or six hours. Afterwards I went to the Leasowes, a farm so called, four or five miles from Hagley.

1785 Friday, March 25 - (Being Good Friday) I hastened to reach Birmingham before the Church service began. A sharper frost I never knew; but indeed our house was hot enough in the evening; and I have not seen a more earnest people. Such an advantage it is to be fully employed. In every place we find labouring men most susceptible of religion. Such a blessing results from that curse: "In the sweat of thy brow shalt thou eat bread."

Tuesday, 29 — At noon I preached in the room at Stafford, to a deeply-affected congregation. This was the more strange, because there are few towns in England less infected with religion than Stafford.

Sunday, November 6 — I preached a funeral sermon for that great and good man, Mr. Fletcher; and most of the congregation felt that God was in the midst of them. In the afternoon I buried the remains of Judith Perry, a lovely young woman, snatched away at eighteen; but she was ripe for the Bridegroom, and went to meet Him in the full triumph of faith.

THE FREE SCHOOL

STRATFORD

SHAKESPEARE'S BIRTHPLACE

ROOM IN WHICH SHAKESPEARE WAS BORN

1786 Wednesday, July 5 — Notice was given, without my knowledge, of my preaching at Belper, seven miles short of Derby. I was nothing glad of this, as it obliged me to quit the turnpike-road, to hobble over a miserable common. The people, gathered from all parts, were waiting. So I went immediately to the market-place; and standing under a large tree, testified: "This is life eternal, to know Thee, the only true God, and Jesus Christ Whom Thou hast sent." The house at Derby was thoroughly filled in the evening.

ANNE HATHAWAY'S COTTAGE

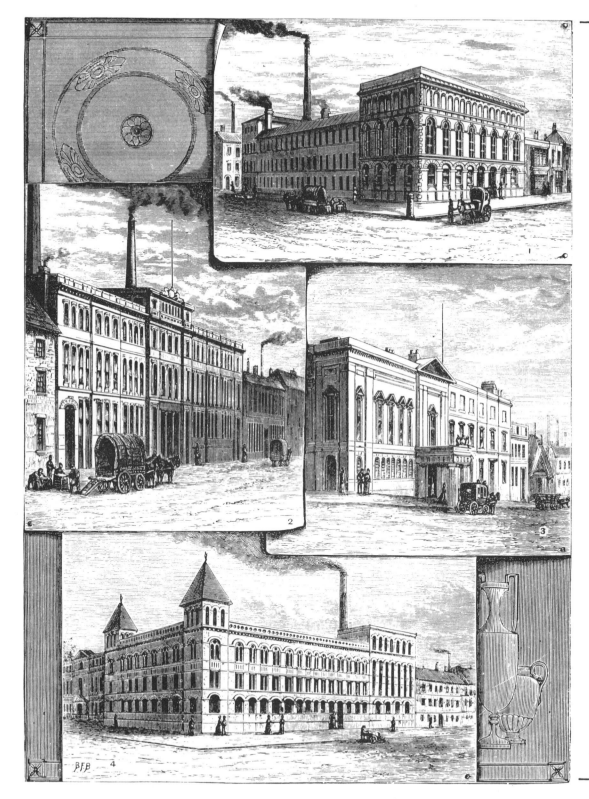

"*In every place we find labouring men most susceptible of religion.*"

Journals,
March 25, 1785 (Birmingham)

BIRMINGHAM MANUFACTORIES

1. MESSRS. OSLER — GLASS WORKS
2. MESSRS. D.F. TAYLER & CO. — PIN AND WIRE WORKS
3. MESSRS. ELKINGTON — ELECTRO-PLATE WORKS
4. MESSRS. PERRY & CO. — STEEL PEN WORKS

ACROSS THE IRISH SEA

THE COLLEEN BAWN ROCK

ARMS OF THE CITY OF DUBLIN

1 N THE MIDDLE of the fifth century St. Patrick, missionary to the Irish, 'came to a certain hill about a mile distant from Ath Cliath, now called Dublin, and . . . is reported to have broken out into this prophecy: "That small village shall hereafter be an eminent city; it shall increase in eminence and dignity, until at length it shall be lifted up unto the throne of the kingdom" ' (Patrick's biographer, Jocelin).

The church founded by Patrick was later strengthened by Columba (521-597), and was to play a vital and stabilising role in the challenges that lay ahead; in the Viking invasions of the ninth and tenth centuries, in the transfer of authority to the English government, and in the upheaval of the 1641 rebellion and the ascendancy of Cromwell.

Ireland produced some outstanding men at the time of Wesley's many visits. A champion of civil and religious liberty was found in 'the Irish Demosthenes', Henry Grattan (1746-1820), whose spellbinding oratory and statesmanship won him acclaim throughout the land. A statue was erected to him at Trinity College, Dublin, as also to Edmund Burke (1730-1797), admired over all Europe for his political exploits, and described by Johnson as 'the first man in England.' Oliver Goldsmith (1728-1774) became revered for his literary achievements, in 'The Vicar of Wakefield,' 'She stoops to Conquer,' and other works.

John Wesley had a love for Ireland, and some of the richest descriptive passages in his journals are reserved for this beautiful land.

1748

STATUE OF BURKE

Tuesday, March 8 – Before one we sailed out of the harbour. Having a gentle gale it soon lulled me fast asleep. I was waked before five by a violent storm: this continued two or three hours longer, and left us within sight of Howth, with a small breeze, which brought us to the Black-Rock about four in the afternoon.

Monday, 14 – I began preaching at five in the morning; an unheard-of thing in Ireland.

Wednesday, 23 – I talked with a warm man, who was always very zealous for the Church, when he was very drunk, and just able to stammer out the Irish proverb, "No gown, no crown." He was quickly convinced, that, whatever we were, he was himself a child of the devil. We left him full of good resolutions, which held several days.

Sunday, April 2 – I hastened on to Athlone. At six I preached from the window of an unfinished house, opposite to the market-house, (which would not have contained one half of the congregation,) on: "Ye know the grace of our Lord Jesus Christ." I scarce ever saw a better-behaved or more attentive congregation. Indeed, so civil a people as the Irish in

STATUE OF GRATTAN

general, I never saw, either in Europe or America.

Thursday, May 12 – I took the straight road from hence to Dublin. Here ... I observed abundance of ruined buildings; but I observed also, that some of them were never finished; and some had been pulled down by those who built them. Such is the amazing fickleness of this people.

1750 Friday, June 15 – We set out at four, and reached Kilkenny, about twenty-five old Irish miles, about noon. This is by far the most pleasant, as well as fruitful country which I have seen in all Ireland. Our way after dinner lay by Dunmore, the seat of the late Duke of Ormond. We rode through the park for about two miles, by the side of which the river runs. I never saw either in England, Holland, or Germany, so delightful a place. The walks, each consisting of four rows of ashes, the tufts of trees sprinkled up and down, interspersed with the smoothest and greenest lawns, are beautiful beyond description.

1752 Friday, October 6 – (Cork). The ship being under sail, we took boat, and came to Cove in the evening. All the inns being full, we lodged at a private house; but we found one inconvenience herein: we had nothing to eat; for our provisions were on board, and there was nothing to be bought in the town ... At length we procured some eggs and bread, and were well contented.

Wednesday 11 – I rode to Cork, once more and was very fully employed all the day. The next morning we returned to Cove, and about noon got out of the harbour. We immediately found the effects of the late storm, the sea still boiling like a pot. The moon set about eight, but the Northern Lights abundantly supplied her place. Soon after God smoothed the face of the deep, and gave us a small fair wind.

Friday, 13 – I read over Pascal's Thoughts. What could possibly induce such a creature as Voltaire to give such an author as this a good word, unless it was that he once wrote a satire? And so his being a satirist might atone even for his being a Christian.

COURTYARD OF THE CASTLE

THE CUSTOM HOUSE, DUBLIN; BUILT 1781 — 1791, SURMOUNTED BY A STATUE OF HOPE

DR. BENJAMIN FRANKLIN (1706 — 1790), AMERICAN DIPLOMAT, STATESMAN AND SCIENTIST. HE WAS TO BECOME A PERSONAL FRIEND OF GEORGE WHITEFIELD

1753 Saturday, February 17 — (Return to London) — From Dr. Franklin's Letters I learned:

1. That electrical fire (or ether) is a species of fire, infinitely finer than any other yet known. 2. That it is diffused, and in nearly equal proportions, through almost all substances. 3. That as long as it is thus diffused, it has no discernible effect. 4. That if any quantity of it be collected together, whether by art or nature, it then becomes visible in the form of fire, and inexpressibly powerful. 5. That it is essentially different from the light of the sun; for it pervades a thousand bodies which light cannot penetrate, and yet cannot penetrate glass, which light pervades so freely. 6. That lightning is no other than electrical fire, collected by one or more clouds. 7. That all the effects of lightning may be performed by the artificial electric fire. 8. That anything pointed, as a spire or tree, attracts the lightning, just as a needle does the electrical fire. 9. That the electrical fire, discharged on a rat or a fowl, will kill it instantly; but discharged on one dipped in water, will slide off, and do it no hurt at all. In like manner, the lightning which will kill a man in a moment, will not hurt him, if he be thoroughly wet. What an amazing scene is here opened for for after-ages to improve upon!

1756 Monday, May 10 — I went forward to Clonmel, the pleasantest town, beyond all comparison, which I have yet seen in Ireland. It has four broad, straight streets of well-built houses, which cross each other in the centre of the town. Close to the walls, on the south side, runs a broad clear river. Beyond this rises a green and fruitful mountain, and hangs over the town. The vale

JOHN WESLEY AT CORK

runs many miles both east and west, and is well cultivated throughout.

Wednesday, June 16 – In the afternoon I rode to Ballingarrane, a town of Palatines, who came over in Queen Anne's time. They retain much of the temper and manners of their own country, having no resemblance of those among whom they live. I found much life among this plain, artless, serious people. The whole town came together in the evening, and praised God for the consolation.

Monday, July 19 – No sooner did we enter Ulster than we observed the difference. The ground was cultivated just as in England; and the cottages not only neat, but with doors, chimneys and windows. Newry, the first town we came to, (allowing for the size,) is built much after the manner of Liverpool. I preached soon after seven to a large congregation, and to great part of them at five in the morning.

Friday, 23 – I rode in the afternoon to Belfast, the largest town in Ulster. Some think it contains near as many people as Limerick; it is far cleaner and pleasanter.

Monday, 26 – I spoke very plain at Lisburn, both to the great vulgar and the small. But between Seceders, old self-conceited Presbyterians, New-Light men, Moravians, Cameronians, and formal Churchmen, it is a miracle of miracles if any here bring forth

BALLYSHANNON

THE SALMONLEAP

fruit to perfection.

The country between Lisburn and Moira is much like Berkshire, having fruitful vales on each side of the road, and well-wooded hills running even with them, at a small distance.

1758 Wednesday, August 2 – I learned two or three rules, very needful for those who sail between England and Ireland: 1. Never pay till you set sail: 2. Go not on board till the Captain goes on board: 3. Send not your baggage on board till you go yourself.

1765 Monday, May 27 – At five we reached Donegal, the county-town. What a wonderful set of county-towns are in this kingdom! Donegal, and five more, would not make up such a town as Islington. Some have twenty houses in them, Mayo three, and Leitrim, I think, not one.

Tuesday, 28 – We breakfasted at Bally-shannon, I believe the largest and pleasantest town in the county . . . In the evening I took my usual stand in the market-house at Sligo; but here how was the scene changed! I have seen nothing like this since my first entrance into the kingdom. Such a total want of good

THE METHODIST COLLEGE, BELFAST

sense, of good manners, yea of common decency, was shown by not a few of the hearers! It is good to visit Sligo after Londonderry: honour and dishonour balance each other. Have we done nothing here yet? Then it is high time to begin, and try if something can be done now. In the two following days I spoke as strongly as I could; and my labour was not in vain. The congregation increased very considerably, and appeared to be of another spirit.

Saturday, June 8 – I rode to Limerick, and found the preaching-house just finished. I liked it the best of any in the kingdom; being neat, yea elegant, yet not gaudy.

1778 Wednesday, April 29 – I returned to Cork and met the classes. O when will even the Methodists learn not to exagger-ate? After all the pompous accounts I had had

THE LAKES OF KILLARNEY

of the vast increase of the society, it is not increased at all; nay it is a little smaller than it was three years ago: and yet many of the members are alive to God.

Friday, June 5 — We went on to Coleraine. As the barracks here are empty, we hired one wing, which, by laying several rooms into one, supplied us with a spacious preaching-house; but it would not contain a third of the congregation; but standing at the door, I had them all before me in the barrack-square.

Saturday, 6 — I was desired to take a ride to the celebrated Giant's Causeway. It lies eleven English miles from Coleraine. When we came to the edge of the precipice, three or four poor boys were ready to hold our horses, and show us the way down. It being dead low water, we could go anywhere, and see everything to the best advantage

Tuesday 9 - We went to Belfast, the largest town in Ulster, said to contain thirty-

thousand souls. The streets are well laid out; are broad, straight, and well-built. The poor-house stands on an eminence, fronting the main street, and having a beautiful prospect on every side over the whole country: the old men, the old women, the male and the female children, are all employed according to their strength; and all their apartments are airy, sweet and clean, equal to anything of the kind I have seen in England. I preached in the evening on one side of the new church, to far the largest congregation I have seen in Ireland.

THE LINEN HALL

BELFAST WAS FAMOUS IN THE SEVENTEETH CENTURY FOR ITS LINEN TRADE, THE LINEN HALL IN DONEGAL SQUARE BEING ERECTED IN 1785 AT A COST OF £10,000. THE BOOM IN SHIP-BUILDING DID NOT BEGIN UNTIL THE NINETEENTH CENTURY

FACTORY HANDS

1787 Wednesday, July 11 —. At five I took an affectionate leave of this loving people; and, having finished all my business here, in the afternoon I went down with my friends, having taken the whole ship, and went on board The Prince of Wales, one of the Parkgate packets. At seven we sailed with a fair, moderate wind.

LONDON OF THE MID-18TH C

BOW CHURCH AND CHEAPSIDE

W HEN THE FIRE OF LONDON broke out in September 1666, a unique opportunity was given to England's greatest architect, Christopher Wren (1632-1723). He re-designed much of the gutted city, including the Custom House, the Royal Exchange, Marlborough House and many churches, notably St. Bride's Fleet Street, St. Mary-le-Bow Cheapside, St. Michael's Cornhill and St. James' Piccadilly, it is, however, St. Paul's Cathedral which best illustrates his creative genius, a masterpiece of grace and harmony, finally completed in 1710, when Wesley would have been seven years old.

A few buildings have survived the ravages of history, including the City's most ancient parish Church, Great St. Helen's in Bishopsgate – the scene of more than one visit by Wesley – and the Tower of London, whose keep, the White Tower, dates back to the eleventh century. Let us then visit London of the mid-eighteenth century, and see it through the eyes of John Wesley.

SIR CHRISTOPHER WREN

PALL MALL ABOUT 1740

1755 Tuesday, December 23 – I was in the robe chamber, adjoining to the House of Lords, when the king put on his robes. His brow was much furrowed with age, and quite clouded with care. And is this all the world can give even to a king? All the grandeur it can afford? A blanket of ermine round his shoulders, so heavy and cumbersome he can scarce move under it! And huge heap of borrowed hair, with a few plates of gold and glittering stones upon his head! Alas, what a bauble is human greatness! And even this will not endure.

1768 Wednesday, December 14 – I saw the Westminster scholars act the "Adelphi" of Terence; an entertainment not unworthy of a Christian. O how do these heathens

GEORGE II — 1683–1760

shame us! Their very comedies contain both excellent sense, the liveliest pictures of men and manners, and so fine strokes of genuine morality, as are seldom found in the writings of Christians.

1770 Saturday, November 10 – I returned to London, and had the melancholy news of Mr. Whitefield's death confirmed by his executors, who desired me to preach his funeral sermon on Sunday, the 18th. In order to write this, I retired to

Lewisham on _Monday;_ and on _Sunday_ following, went to the chapel in Tottenham-court-road. An immense multitude was gathered together from all corners of the town. I was at first afraid that a great part of the congregation would not be able to hear; but it pleased God so to strengthen my voice, that even those at the door heard distinctly. It was an awful season: all were as still as night; most appeared to be deeply affected; and an impression was made on many, which one would hope will not speedily be effaced.

1771 Thursday, February 14 – I went through both the upper and lower rooms of the London workhouse. It contains about an hundred children, who are in as good order as any private family. And the whole house is as clean, from top to bottom, as any gentleman's need be. And why is not every workhouse in London, yea, through the kingdom, in the same order?

CORNHILL: THE EXCHANGE AND LOMBARD STREET

THE MONUMENT

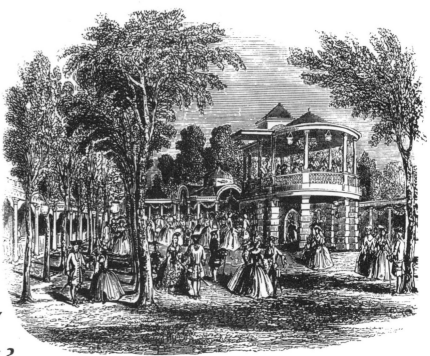

VAUXHALL IN 1751

Where finds Philosophy her
eagle eye,
With which she gazes at
yon burning disk
Undazzled, and detects and
counts his spots?
In London. Where her
implements exact
With which she calculates,
computes and scans
All distance, motion,
magnitude, and now
Measures an atom, and
now girds a world?
In London. Where has commerce
such a mart,
So rich, so throng'd, so drained
and so supplied,
As London,
opulent,
enlarged,
and still
Increasing
London?

William
Cowper
1731 – 1800

HOUSES OF PARLIAMENT FROM THE RIVER
IN WESLEY'S TIME

LONDON BRIDGE JUST BEFORE THE HOUSES WERE PULLED
DOWN IN 1760

HAMPTON COURT: BUILT BY CARDINAL WOLSEY, WHO
LATER GAVE IT TO HENRY VIII. IT CONTINUED A
ROYAL RESIDENCE UNTIL GEORGE II'S REIGN

1775 Sunday, October 8 —
I preached in Moor-
fields to a larger congregation
than usual. Strange that their
curiosity should not be satisfied
yet, after hearing the same thing
near forty years!

Sunday, November 12 —
I was desired to preach, in
Bethnal - green church, a charity
sermon for the widows and
orphans of the soldiers that were
killed in America.

1776 Thursday, December 5 —
I returned to London.
In the way, I read over Mr.
Gray's Works, and his Life
wrote by Mr. Mason. He is an
admirable poet, not much inferior
to either Prior or Pope.

1772 Friday, February 7 — I called on a friend at Hampton
court, who went with me through the house. It struck
me more than anything of the kind I have seen in England; more
than Blenheim-house itself. One great difference is, everything
there appears designedly grand and splendid; here everything is
quite, as it were, natural, and one thinks it cannot be otherwise.
If the expression may be allowed, there is a kind of stiffness runs
through the one, and an easiness through the other. Of pictures
I do not pretend to be a judge; but there is one, by Paul
Rubens, which particularly struck me, both with the design and
the execution of it. It is Zacharias and Elizabeth, with John
the Baptist, two or three years old, coming to visit Mary, and
our Lord sitting upon her knee. The passions are surprisingly
expressed, even in the children; but I could not see either the
decency or common-sense of painting them stark naked:
nothing can defend or excuse this ...

LONDON SHOEBLACK

I have not found any such distress, no, not in the prison of Newgate. One poor man was just creeping out of his sick-bed, to his ragged wife and three little children; who were more than half naked, and the very picture of famine; when one bringing in a loaf of bread, they all ran, seized upon it, and tore it in pieces in an instant. Who would not rejoice that there is another world?

THOMAS GRAY
(1716-1771). AUTHOR OF THE FAMOUS
"ELEGY IN A COUNTRY CHURCHYARD"

GEORGE III (1738 – 1820)
IT WAS IN HIS REIGN THAT
BUCKINGHAM PALACE BECAME
THE MONARCH'S RESIDENCE

1777 Wednesday, January 15 – I began visiting those of our society who lived in Bethnal-green hamlet. Many of them I found in such poverty as few can conceive without seeing it. O why do not all the rich that fear God constantly visit the poor? Can they spend part of their spare time better? Certainly not. . . . Such another scene I saw the next day, in visiting another part of the society.

HANDEL (1685 – 1759). HIS
"WATER MUSIC" WAS FIRST PER-
FORMED AT A ROYAL WATER
PARTY ON THE THAMES. HE
BECAME A NATURALIZED ENG-
LISHMAN IN 1726

Sunday, 26 – I preached again at All Hallows church (Lombard Street), morning and afternoon. I found great liberty of spirit; and the congregation seemed to be much affected. How is this? Do I yet please men? Is the offence of the Cross ceased? It seems, after being scandalous near fifty years, I am at length growing into an honourable man!

'I hate to meet John Wesley: the dog enchants you with his conversation, and then breaks away to go and visit some old woman'

Dr. Samuel Johnson

1779 Sunday, February 28 — Immediately after preaching at Spitalfields, I hastened away to St. Peter's, Cornhill, and declared to a crowded congregation: "God hath given us His Holy Spirit." At four I preached in the new chapel for the benefit of the Reformation Society. This also I trust will be a means of uniting together the hearts of the children of God of various denominations.

1783 Thursday, December 18 — I spent two hours with that great man, Dr. Johnson, who is sinking into the grave by a gentle decay.

1785 Sunday, November 13 — I preached at Shoreditch church. The congregation was very numerous and the collection unusually large.

1786 Tuesday, January 24 — I was desired to go and

DR. JOHNSON AND JOHN WESLEY

hear the King (George III) deliver his speech in the House of Lords. But how agreeably was I surprised! He pronounced every word with exact propriety. I much doubt whether there be any other King in Europe that is so just and natural a speaker.

O may thy virtue guard
thee thro' the roads
Of Drury's mazy courts
and dark abodes!
The harlot's guileful paths
who nightly stand
Where Catherine Street
descends into the
Strand.

John Gay, in 1717

NEWCASTLE AND THE NORTH-

SANDGATE, NEWCASTLE

NEWCASTLE, originally the site of a Roman station, began to assume its present shape under Robert, eldest son of William the Conqueror. The 'New Castle' itself was built by Henry II in the twelfth century on the site of Robert's older structure, and was a formidable fortress indeed.

The city's prominence is due to its position on a tidal river and its immense coal resources; 'Carrying coals to Newcastle' has for long denoted the carrying out of unnecessary actions.

Nearby is Gateshead Fell – swept by the Danish invaders of the ninth century and by the Normans in the eleventh. A February day some seven hundred years on saw John Wesley battling his way through a wintry blizzard on a different kind of mission.

1745 Saturday, February 23 – It was past eight before we got to Gateshead-Fell, which appeared a great pathless waste of white. The snow filling up and covering all the roads, we were at a loss how to proceed; when an honest man of Newcastle overtook and guided us safe into the town.

Many a rough journey have I had before, but one like this I never had; between wind, and hail, and rain, and ice, and snow, and driving sleet, and piercing cold: but it is past: those days will return no more, and are therefore as though they had never been.

'Pain, disappointment, sickness, strife,
whate'er molests or troubles life,
However grievous in its stay,
It shakes the tenement of clay,
When past, as nothing we esteem;
And pain, like pleasure, is a dream.'

Wednesday, September 18 – About five we came to Newcastle, in an acceptable time. We found the generality of the inhabitants in the utmost consternation; news being just

WESLEY ON GATESHEAD-FELL

EAST

ARMS OF NEWCASTLE

arrived, that the morning before, at two o'clock, the Pretender had entered Edinburgh. A great concourse of people were with us in the evening, to whom I expounded the third chapter of Jonah; insisting particularly on that verse, "Who can tell if God will return and repent, and turn away from His fierce anger, that we perish not?"

1757 Monday, June 13 – I proclaimed the love of Christ to sinners, in the market-

GRAINGER STREET, NEWCASTLE

place at Morpeth. Thence we rode to Placey. The society of colliers here may be a pattern to all the societies in England. No person ever misses his band or class: they have no jar of any kind among them; but with one heart and one mind "provoke one another to love and to good works."

Tuesday, 28 – I returned to Newcastle, hoarse and weak. But who can be spent in a better cause?

1777 Monday, April 28 – At one I took coach, and on Wednesday evening preached at Newcastle-upon-Tyne. I love our brethren in the southern counties; but still I find few among

ROYAL ARCADE, NEWCASTLE

THE OLD BRIDGE,
BERWICK-ON-TWEED

to preach in his church.
A keener sermon I
never heard. So all
I have done to
persuade the
people to attend
the church is
overturned at
once! And all
who preach thus,
will drive the
Methodists
from the church,
in spite of all
that I can do.

THE SIDE, NEWCASTLE

them that have the spirit of our northern societies.

1781 *Sunday, June 24* – I preached in the morning at Gateshead-Fell: about noon, at a village called Greenside, ten miles west of Newcastle, to the largest congregation I have seen in the north; many of whom were Roman Catholics. In the evening I preached once more at Garth-Heads, (some thought to the largest congregation that had ever been there,) on those words in the service: "Comfort ye, comfort ye My people, saith your God."

1784 *Saturday, June 19* – In the evening I preached to a large congregation at Scarborough.

Sunday, 20 – The new vicar showed plainly, why he refused those who desired the liberty for me

" I love our brethren
in the southern counties;
but still I find few among
them that have the spirit
of our northern counties."

Journals, April 28, 1777

CAMBRIDGE

ARMS OF THE CITY AND
UNIVERSITY OF CAMBRIDGE

NEWTON'S STATUE IN
TRINITY COLLEGE

C AMBRIDGE (Cantebrig, Grantebrigge), situated in the low Fen country, is a university city stalked by the ghosts of an illustrious past. Today's visitor can walk into the Great Court of Trinity, and see much the same scene as would have confronted a student of the seventeenth century. South of the chapel is the staircase once mounted daily by science's greatest giant, Isaac Newton (1642-1727). The rooms to the west formerly housed England's outstanding geologist, Adam Sedgwick (1785-1873). Nearby are the rooms of the poet Byron (1788-1824). Macaulay the historian studied at Trinity, as also George Herbert, Francis Bacon and Alfred Tennyson. And this from one college among many. A brief tour of the other colleges gives us a similarly tenuous but tangible link with such men as Wilberforce, Cromwell and Pitt; Milton, Gray and Wordsworth; Leland the antiquary and Latimer the martyr, besides a galaxy of archbishops and other divines.

It is undeniable that the town of Cambridge preceded the university, which stemmed largely from the religious orders of the thirteenth century. Nevertheless history forces us to concur with Thomas Fuller's observation of 1655: 'Oxford is a university in a town, Cambridge a town in an university.'

KING'S COLLEGE

BRIDGE AT ST. JOHN'S COLLEGE (FOUNDED 1511)

1762 *Sunday, January 10* — At four we took horse, and reached Grantchester a little before seven. Finding a little company met together, I spent half an hour with them exceedingly comfortably, and, through the blessing of God, I was no more tired when I went to bed than when I arose in the morning.

Monday, 11 — The house was thoroughly filled at five, and that with serious and sensible hearers. I was sorry I had no more time at this place, especially as it was so near Cambridge,

THE LEYS SCHOOL, FOUNDED BY PROMINENT
WESLEYANS IN THE CENTURY AFTER WESLEY

from whence many gentlemen used to come when any clergyman preached. But my work was fixed, so I took horse soon after preaching and rode to a village called Bottishamlode seven miles from Cambridge. Here a large congregation was soon assembled, and I had no sooner named my text, "When they had nothing to pay,

FRANCIS BACON (1561 – 1626)
OF TRINITY COLLEGE. HE BECAME
LORD CHANCELLOR OF ENGLAND

he frankly forgave them both," than a murmur ran through the whole people, and many of them were in tears. This concern increased as I went on, so that none appeared to be unmoved.

1763 Tuesday, October 11 – I rode through miserable roads to Cambridge, and thence to Lakenheath. The next day I reached Norwich, and found much of the presence of God in the congregation, both this evening and the next day.

1784 Monday, December 20 – I went to Hinksworth, where I had the satisfaction of meeting Mr. Simeon,* Fellow of King's College, in Cambridge. He has spent some time with Mr.

* Charles Simeon (1759 - 1836) vicar of Holy Trinity Cambridge
for over 50 years, as influential as they were eventful.

KING'S COLLEGE AND CLARE GARDEN

Fletcher, at Madeley: two kindred souls; much resembling each other, both in fervour of spirit, and in the earnestness of their address. He gave me the pleasing information, that there are three parish churches in Cambridge wherein true scriptural religion is preached; and several young gentlemen who are happy partakers of it. I preached in the evening on Galatians vi. 14.

1787 Tuesday, October 30 – I went down to Miss Harvey's, at Hinxworth in Hertfordshire. Mr. Simeon, from Cambridge, met me there; who breathes the very spirit of Mr. Fletcher.

GATEWAY, JESUS COLLEGE
FOUNDED 1496: FORMERLY A
BENEDICTINE NUNNERY

James I on a visit to the University, said " that if he lived at the University he would pray at King's, eat at Trinity, and study at Jesus."

INTERIOR, KING'S COLLEGE CHAPEL

YORK AND THE BATTLEFIELDS

SINCE EARLY TIMES York and its surrounds have set the stage for some of England's fiercest fighting, York itself having been chosen by the Romans as their strategic northern centre, Eboracum. With the Roman withdrawal in 410, the gates were opened for Barbarian incursions from the north. The devastation must have been great, for when King Edwin was baptised in York on Easter Day, 627, no consecrated building was in existence for the ceremony.

After successive struggles between Mercia and Northumbria for control of Yorkshire (Deira), the next major conflict reached its climax in 1066 at the Battle of Stamford Bridge, where Harold Hardrada and Earl Tostig were annihilated by Harold of England, who in turn was overthrown by William the Conqueror. In 1138 David of Scotland met with defeat at the Battle of the Standard near Northallerton, and in 1318 the areas surrounding Boroughbridge, Scarborough and Skipton were flattened by the forces of Robert the Bruce.

Of the many further struggles, none can compare in importance with the Wars of the Roses that settled the succession to the throne in the fifteenth century, and, of course, the Civil War two centuries later. This latter struggle, coupled with the 'Bloodless Revolution' of 1688 and the subsequent Bill of Rights accepted by William and Mary, firmly established the principle that government must be by consent of the governed.

1766 *Saturday, July 19 – I took a view of Beverley Minster, such a parish church as has scarce its fellow in England. It is a most beautiful as well as stately building, both within and without, and is kept more nicely clean than any cathedral which I have seen in the kingdom. About one I preached at Pocklington, (though my strength was much exhausted,) and in the evening at York.*

Sunday, 20 – After preaching at eight, I went to St. Saviourgate church. Towards the close of the prayers the rector sent the sexton to tell me the pulpit was at my

SANDSIDE, SCARBOROUGH

service. I preached on the conclusion of the Gospel for the day: "Not every one that saith unto Me, Lord, Lord, shall enter into the kingdom of heaven; but he that doeth the will of my Father which is in heaven." I did not see one person laugh or smile, though we had an elegant congregation.

1774 *Tuesday, June 14 – We crossed over the enormous mountains into lovely Wenaudale; the largest by far of all the dales, as well as the most beautiful... As I rode through the town, the people stood staring on every side, as if we had been a company of*

ARMS OF THE CITY AND SEE OF YORK

monsters. I preached in the street, and they soon ran together, young and old, from every quarter. I reminded the elder, of their having seen me thirty years before, when I preached in Wensley church; and enforced once more: "Believe in the Lord Jesus Christ, and thou shalt be saved ..."

Hence we hasted to Richmond, where I preached in a kind of square. All the Yorkshire militia were there; and so were their officers, who kept them in awe, so that they behaved with decency.

1776 Monday, June 24 – I went on to Scarborough. I think the preaching-house here is the most elegant of any square room which we have in England; and we had as elegant a congregation: but they were as attentive as if they had been Kingswood colliers.

Tuesday, July 2 – I went to York. The house was full enough in the evening, while

I pointed the true and the false way of expounding those important words: "Ye are saved through faith."

MICKLEGATE BAR, YORK
IN THE TIME OF THE CIVIL WAR

Wednesday, 3 – I preached about noon at Tadcaster, with an uncommon degree of freedom; which was attended with a remarkable blessing. A glorious work is dawning here, against which nothing can prevail ...

1780 Sunday, June 4 – The service began about ten at Staveley, near Boroughbridge. Mr. Hartley, the rector, read prayers. But the church would scarce contain half the congregation; so that I was obliged to stand upon a tombstone, both morning and afternoon. In the evening I preached at Boroughbridge, to a numerous congregation; and all were attentive except a few soldiers, who seemed to understand nothing of the matter.

1781 Wednesday, August 15 – I went to Sheffield. In the afternoon I took a view of the chapel lately built by the Duke of Norfolk. One may safely say, there is none like it in the three kingdoms; nor, I suppose, in the world. It is a stone building, an octagon, about eighty feet diameter. A cupola, which is at a great height, gives some, but not much, light. A little more is given by four small windows, which are under the galleries. The pulpit is movable: it rolls upon wheels; and is shifted once a quarter, that all the pews may face it in their turns: I presume the first contrivance of the kind in Europe.

WHITBY

SHEFFIELD: CASTING CRUCIBLE STEEL

1. CASTING
2. WATCHING THE FURNACE
3. FUNNEL FOR FILLING POTS IN THE FURNACE

" Off with his head, and set it on York Gate, So York may overlook the town of York."

Queen Margaret, referring to Richard, Duke of York in the Wars of the Roses – Shakespeare's Henry VI

YORK MINSTER

AFTER ITS DESTRUCTION IN THE NORMAN CONQUEST, IT WAS RECONSTRUCTED IN VARIOUS STAGES, BEING FINALLY RECONSECRATED ON FEBRUARY 3, 1472

THE OLD BATH ROAD AND

WITH THE EIGHTEENTH CENTURY began Bath's golden era – enhanced by two royal visits (in 1734 and 1738), by the work of the two architects Wood (both named John), and by the city's most flamboyant figure and Master of Ceremonies, Richard 'Beau' Nash (born 1674) – voted by popular acclaim as 'King of Bath'. Many made the pilgrimage, as much for the amusements provided as for the healing properties of the mineral springs, which had been well-known to the Romans. Indeed it was the Romans who had constructed the great Bath Road that ran from London, through the Marlborough Downs, and on to the West.

Travellers to Bath would find Marlborough a convenient halting place. The Castle Inn (converted from the old Marlborough Castle) became famous among experienced pilgrims, William Pitt himself spending several weeks there during a time of crisis. Eventually, with the arrival of the Great Western Railway, the Castle Inn went out of business. Today it serves as the oldest boarding house of Marlborough's great public school.

Further west and south of Bath are some of England's most romantic sites – Glastonbury with its numerous legends; the marshes of Athelney, which once sheltered Alfred from the Danes; and Corfe Castle which, for long, stood sentry over the Isle of Purbeck. We can imagine Wesley as he travelled along the Old Bath Road, with the aim of re-opening England's West Country for the Christian faith.

"YOU, MR. NASH, TAKE CARE OF YOUR BODY; WE TAKE CARE OF OUR SOULS..."

1739 *Tuesday, June 5* – There was great expectation at Bath of what a noted man was to do to me there; and I was much entreated not to preach, because no one knew what might happen. By this report I also gained a much larger audience, among whom were many of the rich and great. I told them plainly, the Scripture had concluded them all under sin: high and low, rich and poor, one with another. Many of them seemed to be a little surprised, and were sinking apace into seriousness, when their champion appeared, and, coming close to me, asked by what authority I did these things. I replied, "By the authority of Jesus Christ, conveyed to me by the (now) Archbishop of Canterbury, when he laid hands upon me, and said, 'Take thou

THE WEST

ARMS OF BATH

BATH, FROM NEAR THE ABBEY CEMETERY.

replied, "Sir, leave him to me: let an old woman answer him. You, Mr. Nash, take care of your body; we take care of our souls; for the food of our souls we come here." He replied not a word, but walked away.

1747 Sunday, June 21 — After preaching at the chapel in the afternoon, I set out for Brentford with Robert Swindells. The next day we reached Marlborough, where one in the room beneath us was swearing desperately. Mr. Swindells stepped down and put into his hand the paper entitled, "Swear not at all." He

THE CASTLE INN, MARLBOROUGH, LATER THE OLD SCHOOL HOUSE, 200 YARDS FROM THE BATH ROAD

authority to preach the Gospel.'" He said, "This is contrary to Act of Parliament: this is a conventicle." I answered, "Sir, ... here is no shadow of sedition; therefore it is not contrary to that Act." He replied, "I say it is; and beside, your preaching frightens people out of their wits." "Sir, did you ever hear me preach?" "No." "How then can you judge of what you never heard?" "Sir, by common report." "Common report is not enough. Give me leave, Sir, to ask, Is not your name Nash?" "My name is Nash." "Sir, I dare not judge of you by common report: I think it not enough to judge by." Here he paused awhile, and, having recovered himself, said, "I desire to know what this people comes here for:" on which one

thanked him, and promised to swear no more. And he did not while he was in the house. We took horse at three, breakfasted at Chippenham, and dined at Kingswood; whence I walked to Bristol.

1750 Friday, August 31 – Setting out early, we reached Collumpton in the evening; but as I was not expected, the congregation was small.

Sunday, September 2 – I rode to Tiverton. At eight I preached to twice as many people as were present when I was here before; but even this congregation was doubled at one and at five. The meadow was then full from side to side, and many stood in the gardens and orchards round.

Monday, 3 – We rode to Shaftesbury, where I preached, between six and seven, to a serious and quiet congregation. We had another happy opportunity at five in the morning, when abundance of people were present. I preached, at noon, in the most riotous part of the town, just where four ways met; but none made any noise, or spoke one word, while I called "the wicked to forsake his way."

MOUNDS AND
MONUMENTS
IN WILTSHIRE:

THE STONE RING
AT AVEBURY

SILBURY HILL

THE DEVIL'S DEN

'THE GREAT STONES OF
STONEHENGE:

"COME THITHER, AND
FIND THEM AS PRODIGIOUS
AS ANY TALES I HAVE
HEARD OF THEM, AND
WORTH GOING THIS
JOURNEY TO SEE."

SAMUEL PEPYS

Soon after I was sat down, a constable came, and said, "Sir, the Mayor discharges you from preaching in this borough any more." I replied, "While King George gives me leave to preach, I shall not ask leave of the Mayor of Shaftesbury."

1774 Monday, October 10 — I preached at Salisbury; and on Tuesday, 11, set out for the Isle of Purbeck. When we came to Corfe-castle, the evening being quite calm and mild, I preached in a meadow near the town, to a deeply-attentive congregation, gathered from all parts of the island. I afterwards met the society, artless and teachable, and full of good desires. But few of them yet have got any farther than to "see men as trees walking."

Wednesday, 12 — I preached to a large congregation at five, who seemed quite athirst for for instruction. Afterwards we took a walk over the remains of the castle, so bravely defended in the last century, against all the power of the Parliament forces, by the widow of the Lord

Chief Justice Banks. It is one of the noblest ruins I ever saw: the walls are of an immense thickness, defying even the assaults of time, and were formerly surrounded by a deep ditch. The house, which stands in the middle, on the very top of the rock, has been a magnificent structure. Some time since the proprietor fitted up some rooms on the south-west of this, and laid out a little garden, commanding a large prospect, pleasant beyond description ...

About noon I preached at Langton, three or four miles from Corfe-castle, to a large and deeply serious congregation. In the evening I preached in a meadow, near Swanage, to a still larger congregation.

SALISBURY CATHEDRAL, BUILT 1220-1266

SENTINEL OVER PURBECK: CORFE CASTLE

1776 Wednesday, March 6 – I went down to Taunton, and at three in the afternoon opened the new preaching-house. The people showed great eagerness to hear. Will they at length know the day of their visitation?

1778 Tuesday, September 1 – I went to Tiverton. I was musing here on what I heard a good man say long since, – "Once in seven years I burn all my sermons; for it is a shame if I cannot write better sermons now than I could seven years ago."

Whatever others can do, I really cannot. I cannot write a better sermon on the Good Steward than I did seven years ago... Forty years ago I knew and preached every Christian doctrine which I preach now.

Tuesday, 8 – In the evening I stood on one side of the market-place at Frome, and declared to a very numerous congregation: "His commandments are not grievous." They stood as quiet as those at Bristol, a very few excepted; most of whom were, by the courtesy of England, called gentlemen. How much inferior to the keelmen and colliers!

THE MARKET PLACE, FROME

1782 Sunday, August 18 – (Exeter) I was much pleased with the decent behaviour of the whole congregation at the cathedral; as also with the solemn music at the post-communion, one of the finest compositions I ever heard. The bishop, inviting me to dinner, I could not but observe, 1. The lovely situation of the palace, covered with trees, and as rural and retired as if it was quite in the country. 2. The plainness of the furniture, not costly or showy, but just fit for a Christian bishop. 3. The dinner, sufficient but not redundant; plain and good, but not delicate...

We set out early in the morning, Monday, 19, and in the afternoon came to Plymouth. I preached in the evening, and at five and twelve on Tuesday, purposing to preach in the square at the dock in the evening; but the rain prevented.

1784 Thursday, September 23 – I preached at Paulton about one; and at Pensford in the evening. The gentleman at Chew-Magna having sent me word I was welcome to preach in the church, I went thither the next morning; but they now sent me word they had changed

BATH — THE MOST FLOURISHING AND FASHIONABLE OF THE 18TH-CENTURY ENGLISH SPAS

to new worlds, till I go to the world of spirits.

1785 Monday, February 28 — The diligence reached Sarum about eight in the evening. About nine we left it. So keen a frost, I hardly ever felt before: and our carriage let in the air on all sides, so that we hardly could preserve life. However, soon after five on Tuesday evening we got to Exeter.

Friday, March 4 — I took a walk through the Royal Hospital for sick and wounded sailors. I never saw anything of the kind so complete: every part is so convenient, and so admirably neat. But there is nothing superfluous, and nothing purely ornamental, either within or without. There seems to be nothing wanting, but a man full of faith and zeal, to watch

SIR JOSHUA REYNOLDS (1723–1792)
OF PLYMPTON, DEVON: THE MOST
PROMINENT FIGURE IN THE ENGLISH
SCHOOL OF PAINTING

their minds; so I preached in our own preaching-house....

Thursday, September 30 — I had a long conversation with John M'Geary, one of our American preachers, just come to England. He gave a pleasing account of the work of God there, continually increasing, and vehemently im-portuned me to pay one more visit to America before I die. Nay, I shall pay no more visits

GLASTONBURY: HOME OF SAINTS AND LEGENDS
THE BURIAL PLACE OF KING ARTHUR

over the souls of the poor patients, and teach them to improve their affliction.

In the evening I preached to a large congregation at Plymouth; and it pleased God to give me uncommon liberty in describing the power of faith.

What a blessed proof of this has there been here, since I was in the town before!

1786 Monday, September 11 – (Bath) Leaving the society here well united together, I went on...

THE OLD BATH ROAD

(from a Marlborough College School song)

Strong and true, on its western stages,
Girt by downland and tree-clad hill,
Strong and true, as in by-gone ages,
The old Bath Road fares onward still.
And strong and true, the young with the older,
Stands the School, our youth's abode,
Side by side, and shoulder to shoulder,
Guarding the flanks of the old Bath Road.

Old Bath Road you have conquered regions
Fenced with forest and sunk in swamp,
Rung 'neath the tramp of Roman legions,
Borne the pageant of Roman pomp.
But to-day from city and town and shire,
Hither you bring to your cherished school
Youth, that may learn the things that are higher
Than Norman splendour and Roman Rule.

OVER THE WELSH

THE TORRENT WALK

THE MOUNTAINOUS country of Wales, with its rocky coasts, its rivers, moorlands and coalmines, has known the power of Christianity since the Roman era. At times the flame of devotion has burned low, only to be revived in periods of great spiritual fervour through leaders such as David (c.520-589), patron saint of Wales, William Morgan (c.1547-1604) who produced the first Welsh Bible, and Howell Harris (1713-1773), associate of Wesley, and leader of the eighteenth-century Evangelical Revival in Wales.

Wesley, though a visitor to Wales, took no real part in the organising of the Methodist societies, leaving Harris to develop the work in an indigenous – and sometimes erratic – direction. At the height of the revival, Wesley complained, 'They start up, and cry, "Glory! glory!" perhaps twenty times together. Just so do the French Prophets, and very lately the Jumpers in Wales, bring the real work into contempt' (Journals, April 3rd, 1786). Even so, the revival was to affect every part of the Welsh culture, becoming something of a real folk-movement in the country.

1740 _Monday, April 7_ – At the pressing instance of Howell Harris, I again set out for Wales. In the evening I preached "repentance and remission of sins," at Lanvachas, three miles from the New Passage.

1747 _Wednesday, August 5_ – Taking horse early in the morning, we rode over the rough mountains of Radnorshire and Montgomeryshire into Merionethshire. In the evening I was surprised with one of the finest prospects, in its kind, that ever I saw in my life. We rode in a green vale, shaded with rows of trees, which made an arbour for several miles. The river laboured along on our left hand, through broken rocks of every size, shape and colour. On the other side of the river, the mountain rose to an immense height, almost

DOLGELLY, MERIONETHSHIRE

MOUNTAINS

perpendicular: and yet the tall straight oaks stood, rank above rank, from the bottom to the very top; only here and there, where the mountain was not so steep, were interposed pastures or fields of corn. At a distance, as far as the eye could reach, as it were by way of contrast,

"A mountain huge upreared
Its broad bare back,"

with vast rugged rocks hanging over its brow, that seemed to nod portending ruin.

HARLECH CASTLE

1756 <u>Friday, August 13</u> – Before one we reached Bangor, the situation of which is delightful beyond expression. Here we saw a large and handsome cathedral, but no trace of the good old monks of Bangor; so many hundreds of whom fell at once to cruelty and revenge. The country from hence to Penmaen-Mawr is far pleasanter than any garden. Mountains of every shape and size, vales clothed with grass or corn, woods and smaller tufts of trees, were continually varying on the one hand, as was the sea prospect on the other. Penmaen-Mawr itself rises almost perpendicular to an enormous height from the sea.

HOWELL HARRIS

1763 <u>Saturday, August 20</u> – We took horse at four, and rode through one of the pleasantest countries in the world. When we came to Trecastle, we had rode fifty miles in Monmouthshire and Brecknockshire; and I will be bold to say, all England does not afford such a line of fifty miles length, for fields, meadows, brooks and gently-rising mountains, fruitful to the very top. Carmarthenshire, into which we came soon

A WELSH PEASANT WOMAN

after, has at least as fruitful a soil; but it is not so pleasant, because it has fewer mountains, though abundance of brooks and rivers. About five I preached on the green at Carmarthen, to a large number of deeply attentive people.

1771 I rode on _Thursday, (August) 22,_ to Dala, a little village at the mouth of Milford-Haven ... I told them just what I thought. It went as a sword to their hearts. They felt the truth, and wept bitterly.

Friday, 23 — I preached at noon, to a lovely congregation of plain, artless people, at Houghton; and in the town-hall at Pembroke, in the evening, to many rich and elegant hearers.

Tuesday, 27 — We crept through a right Welsh road, and reached Oxwych between twelve and one. The congregation had waited for some time; so I began without delay. The road to Swansea was a little better; so I reached the town in time, and at six preached in the yard, as our room would contain hardly a third of the people.

1781 _Tuesday, May 1_ – I rode to St. David's, seventeen measured miles from Haverford. I was surprised to find all the land, for the last nine or ten

BANGOR

miles, so fruitful and well-cultivated. What a difference is there between the westernmost parts of England, and the westernmost parts of Wales!

"Mountains of every shape and size, vales clothed with grass or corn, woods and smaller tufts of trees, were continually varying on the one hand, as was the sea prospect on the other."

(Road between Bangor and Penmaen-Mawr)

Journals, August 13, 1751

THE LLEDR VALLEY, TYPICAL OF THE COUNTRYSIDE THAT CAPTIVATED WESLEY ON HIS TRAVELS

NORWICH – CITY OF

ARM OF THE CITY
AND SEE OF NORWICH

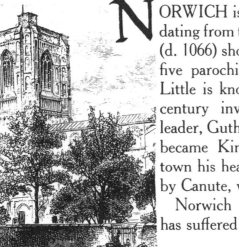

ST. PETER MANCROFT,
NORWICH'S FINEST CHURCH

NORWICH is a city of churches – documents dating from the time of Edward the Confessor (d. 1066) show that even then it 'had twenty-five parochial churches, if not more . . .' Little is known of Norwich until the ninth century invasions of the Danish, whose leader, Guthrum (later baptised as Athelstan) became King of East Anglia, making the town his headquarters. It was also possessed by Canute, who strengthened its castle.

Norwich has had an eventful history. It has suffered various sieges; it was plundered and burnt by the Dauphin's army in 1216; it prospered through the arrival of Flemish weavers in the fourteenth century, but received a sharp set-back in 1348-9, when a third of its inhabitants were wiped out by the Black Death; many of its townsmen were involved in Wat Tyler's uprising of 1381; it suffered severely from fires in 1507 and 1509; and Thomas Bilney, a Norwich divine, was burnt at the stake in 1531, during the Marian persecution.

The superb cathedral, with a spire second only in height to that of Salisbury, was largely completed in the twelfth century.

A GENERAL VIEW OF NORWICH

1775

Saturday, December 2 – (Norwich) I procured "the History of Norwich," published but a few years since.

In the evening a large mob gathered at the door of the preaching-house, the captain of which struck many (chiefly women) with a large stick. Mr. Randal going out to see what was the matter, he struck him with it in the face. But he was soon secured, and carried before the mayor; who, knowing him to be a notorious offender, against whom one or two warrants were then lying, sent him to gaol without delay.

Tuesday, 5 – We set out a little before day, and reached Lynn in the afternoon. In the evening, the new house would hardly contain one half of the congregation.

Wednesday, 6 – I visited many of those that remained with us, and those that had left us since they had learned a new doctrine. I did not dispute, but endeavoured to soften their spirits, which had been sharpened to a high degree. In the evening the chapel

CHURCHES

NELSON (1755 – 1805)
FOR A WHILE A PUPIL AT
THE GRAMMAR SCHOOL

was quite too small: and yet even those who could not get in were silent: a circumstance which I have seldom observed in any other part of England.

Saturday, 16 – Today I read Dr. Beattie's poems; certainly one of the best poets of the age. He wants only the ease and simplicity of Mr. Pope. – I know one, and only one, that has it.

1779 Thursday, February 18 – I preached at Lowestoft, where is a great awakening, especially among youth and children; several of whom, between twelve and sixteen years of age, are a pattern to all about them.

Sunday, 21 – I returned to Norwich, and took an exact account of the society. I wish all our preachers would be accurate in their accounts, and rather speak under than above the truth. I had heard again and again of the increase of the society. And what is the naked truth? Why, I left in it two hundred and two members; and I find one hundred and seventy-nine! At twelve I took coach, and in the morning reached London.

NORWICH MARKET-PLACE, THE MOST LONG-STANDING OF ENGLAND'S MARKETS, DATES FROM BEFORE THE NORMAN CONQUEST. IT IS IN USE MOST DAYS AT THE PRESENT TIME.

1781 <u>Sunday, October 28</u> — (Norwich)
I preached at Bear-Street to a large congregation, most of whom had never seen my face before.

<u>Tuesday, 30</u> — I went to Wells, a considerable sea-port, twelve miles from Fakenham, where also Miss Franklin had opened a door, by preaching abroad, though at the peril of her life...
At two in the afternoon I preached at Walsingham, a place famous for many generations. Afterwards I walked over what is left of the famous Abbey, the east end of which is still standing. We then went to the Priary; the cloisters and chapel whereof are almost entire. Had there been a grain of virtue or public spirit in Henry the Eighth, these noble buildings need not have run to ruin.

WALSINGHAM ABBEY

PULL'S FERRY, NORWICH, A 15TH CENTURY WATERGATE

Norwich — "the suburbs are large, the prospects sweete . . ."

English diarist, John Evelyn, in 1671

THE ENDURING THAMES

WINDSOR CASTLE

ALTHOUGH the mighty jet airliners of the world's busiest airport pass overhead by the minute, there is much to remind us that a survey of the Thames Basin is virtually a survey of England's history. The finest vantage point is perhaps the royal residence itself, Windsor Castle, which owes its present magnificence largely to Edward III (1312-1377). From the keep can be seen a vista stretching across several counties.

Nearby is Runnymede, where the Magna Carta was signed over seven hundred and fifty years ago. Across the river is the famous school founded by Henry VI in 1440 – Eton; where England's greatest soldier Wellington was educated. To the south, over the beautiful Surrey Downs, lies Leith Hill, between Dorking and Ockley – site of a national victory over the Danes in 857.

It is the winding Thames that has seen it all; the pageantry, the fluctuations of power, the unfolding drama of Monarchy and people – and, through men of faith like Wesley, the maintaining of Christianity's flame within the realm of Merry England.

"THE PLAYING FIELDS OF ETON"

1742 Tuesday, September 28 – A little before twelve I came to Windsor. I was soon informed that a large number of the rabble had combined together, and declared, again and again, there should be no preaching there that day. In order to make all sure, they had provided gunpowder enough and other things some days before. But Burnham Fair coming between, they agreed to go thither first and have a little diversion there.

Accordingly they went, and bestowed a few of their crackers upon their brother-mob at Burnham. But these, not being Methodists, did not take it well, turned upon them, and gave them chase. They took shelter in an house. But that would not serve; for those without soon forced a way in, and seized on as many as they could find, who, upon information made, were sent to jail. The rest ran away, so that when I came none hindered or interrupted.

1743 Saturday, January 29 – I...came to Reading on Saturday, and to Windsor on Sunday morning. Thence I walked over to Egham, where Mr. —— preached one of the most miserable sermons I ever heard: stuffed so full of dull, senseless improbable lies of those he complimented with the title of "False Prophets."

I preached at one, and endeavoured to rescue the poor text (Matt. vii. 15) out of so bad hands. About four I left Egham, and at eight in the evening met with a joyful congregation at the Foundery.

1764 Thursday, January 12 — I preached at Mitcham, and in the afternoon rode to Dorking; but the gentleman to whose house I was invited seemed to have no desire I should preach. So that evening I had nothing to do. Friday the 13th I went at noon into the street, and in a broad place not far from the market place proclaimed "the grace of our Lord Jesus Christ." At first two or three little children were the whole of my congregation; but it quickly increased, though the air was sharp, and the ground exceeding wet; and all behaved well but three or four grumbling men, who stood so far off that they disturbed none but themselves.

1771 Saturday, October 5 — I set out at two. About ten some of our London friends met me at Cobham, with whom I took a walk in the neighbouring gardens, inexpressibly pleasant, through the variety of hills and dales, and the admirable contrivance of the whole.

Wednesday, 16 — I preached at South-Leigh. Here it was that I preached my first sermon, six-and-forty years ago. One man was in my present audience who heard it. Most of the rest are gone to their long home. After preaching at Witney in the evening, I met the believers apart, and was greatly refreshed among them.

THE THAMES AT RICHMOND BRIDGE

SOUTH-LEIGH CHURCH
WHERE WESLEY'S FIRST SERMON
WAS PREACHED

1775 <u>Wednesday, October 18</u> - I returned to Newbury. Some of our friends informed me, there were many red-hot patriots here; so I took occasion to give a strong exhortation, to "fear God, and honour the king."

1776 <u>Wednesday, May 1</u> - In

travelling through Berkshire . . . I diligently made two enquiries: the first was, concerning the increase or decrease of the people; the second, concerning the increase or decrease of trade. As to the latter, it is, within these last two years, amazingly increased; in several branches in such a manner as has not been known in the memory of man: such is the fruit of the entire civil and religious liberty which all England now enjoys! And as to the former, not only in every city and large town, but in every village and hamlet, there is no decrease, but a very large and swift increase. One sign of this is the swarms of little children which we see in every place.

1777 <u>Monday, March 10</u> - In the evening I preached at Reading. How many years were we beating the air at this town! Stretching out our hands to a people as stupid as oxen! But it is not so at present.

<u>Friday, 28</u> - I received an affectionate message from a great man. — But I shall not wonder if the wind changes.

<u>Sunday, April 6</u> - I began a journey through some of our societies, to desire their assistance towards the expense of the new chapel (City Road).

HIGH STREET, DORKING

READING, FROM CAVERSHAM HILL
AN OLD PRINT

Composed upon Westminster Bridge

Earth has not anything to show more fair:
Dull would he be of soul who could pass by
A sight so touching in its majesty:
This City now doth, like a garment, wear
The beauty of the morning; silent, bare,
Ships, towers, domes, theatres, and temples lie
Open unto the fields, and to the sky;
All bright and glittering in the smokeless air.
Never did sun more beautifully steep
In his first splendour, valley, rock, or hill;
Ne'er saw I, never felt, a calm so deep!
The river glideth at his own sweet will:
Dear God! the very houses seem asleep;
And all that mighty heart is lying still!

WILLIAM WORDSWORTH 1770-1850

1786 Thursday, September 7 — In the evening I preached at Newbury. It rained and blew vehemently; yet the house was thoroughly filled; and I found uncommon liberty in pushing the inquiry: "Who of you are building on the sand, and who upon a rock?"

THE BUILDING OF WESTMINSTER BRIDGE

" But thank God! The Thames is between me and the Duchess of Queensbury."

Horace Walpole, 1717-1797

THE QUADRANGLE, ETON SCHOOL
FOUNDED BY KING HENRY VI IN 1440

THE LAST YEARS

A S JOHN WESLEY entered the last three years of his life, it appeared that his ministry had at last met with commendation from virtually every quarter. Honours were heaped upon him wherever he travelled. His visits to various parts of the country would be proclaimed as public holidays. For over fifty years the people of England had felt the force of what has been described as 'the single most influential Protestant leader of the English speaking world since the Reformation' (John Wesley, by Stanley Ayling). Nearly a quarter of a million miles had been covered on horseback, and some forty thousand sermons had been preached – a rate of fifteen a week.

Although Wesley's contemporary evangelist Whitefield may have been the more compelling preacher, there is little doubt that Wesley left the more permanent mark on society – and this must be attributed to his organising genius under which chapels and classes mushroomed all over the land.

Wesley preached his last sermon in Mr. Belson's house at Leatherhead on February 23rd, 1791; wrote his last letter the following day, in which he encouraged William Wilberforce in his campaign against the slave traffic; and died in his own house, in City Road, on March 2nd. He was buried in the City Road chapel graveyard on March 9th.

1789 Tuesday, February 24 – Mr. Wilberforce called upon me, and we had an agreeable and useful conversation. What a blessing is it to Mr. Pitt to have such a friend as this!

Tuesday, July 28 – The Conference began: about a hundred preachers were present, and never was our Master more eminently present with us. The case of separation from the Church was largely considered, and we were all unanimous against it.

Sunday, August 16 – (Plymouth). In the morning, I believe, we had not less than six hundred communicants; but they were all admirably well-behaved, as if they indeed discerned the Lord's body. But when I preached in the

INTERVIEW BETWEEN WESLEY AND WILBERFORCE

WESLEY PREACHING — HIS LAST SERMON

afternoon, the house would not hold half the congregation. I chose the space adjoining the south side of the house, capable of containing some thousands of people. Besides, some hundreds sat on the ridge of the rock which ran along at my left hand. I preached on part of the Gospel for the day: "He beheld the city and wept over it."

Tuesday, December 8 — (Chatham). We took a walk in the dock-yard. In the evening I preached in the elegant house at Brompton; but it is already far too small. The people flock in on every side, to hear peacefully the Gospel.

Monday, December 14 — (Canterbury). It pleased God to

give me uncommon liberty of spirit; as also at Dover the next evening, where the new house, large as it is, was far too small, so that many could not get in.

Sunday, December 27 — (London). I preached in St. Luke's, our parish church, in the afternoon, to a very numerous congregation, on: "The Spirit and the Bride say, Come." So are the tables turned, that I have now more invitations to preach in churches than I can accept of.

1790 Friday, January 1 — I am now an old man, decayed from head to foot. My eyes are dim; my right hand shakes much, my mouth is hot and dry every morning; I have a lingering fever almost every day; my motion is weak and slow. However, blessed be God, I do not slack my labour: I can preach and write still.

THE TREE AT WINCHELSEA, UNDER WHICH WESLEY PREACHED HIS LAST SERMON IN THE OPEN AIR

WESLEY AT 63

Friday, April 9 -
We went to Wigan, for many years proverbially called Wicked Wigan: but it is not now what it was: the inhabitants in general have taken a softer mould. The house in the evening was more than filled; and all that could get in seemed to be greatly affected, while I strongly applied our Lord's words: "I will; be thou clean."

Sunday, September 5 - This day I cut off that vile custom, I know not when or how it began, of preaching three times a day by the same preacher, to the same congregation; enough to weary out both the bodies and minds of the speaker, as well as his hearers.

Thursday, October 7 - I went over to that poor skeleton of ancient Winchelsea. It is beautifully situated on the top of a steep hill, and was regularly built in broad streets, crossing each other, and encompassing a very large square; in the midst of which was a large church, now in ruins. I stood under a large tree, on the side of it, and called to most of the inhabitants of the town: "The Kingdom of heaven is at hand; repent, and believe the Gospel."

Sunday, October 24 - I explained to a numerous congregation in Spitalfields church, "the whole armour of God." St. Paul's, Shadwell, was still more crowded in the afternoon, while I enforced that important truth: "One thing is needful;" and I hope many, even then, resolved to choose the better part.

JOHN WESLEY DIED AT THE AGE OF 88 ON MARCH 2ND, 1791

TABLE
of
PLACES, PEOPLE AND ILLUSTRATIONS

PLACES	PEOPLE	ILLUSTRATIONS
	OXFORD	
St. Mary's Church — Christ Church Finstock — St. John's College Trinity Gardens — Magdalene Water Walks — White Walk, Oxford	John Wesley, Fellow of Lincoln College, Oxford Peter Böhler	Gateway of St. Mary's Church, Oxford Bocardo Prison PLATE: Oxford from Headington Hill
	LONDON	
Aldersgate Street — Islington Blackheath — Wapping Upper Moorfields Kennington Common — Lambeth	Dr. Samuel Johnson Bishop Butler Daniel Defoe George Whitefield	Dr. Samuel Johnson Islington in the 18th Century St. Paul's Cathedral George Whitefield PLATE: Kensington Gardens Kennington — Thames Embankment
	LINCOLNSHIRE	
Epworth Mighton-Car — Awkborough Barrow — Purrysberg, Georgia Grimsby — Boston The Minster, Lincoln	Alfred the Great Samuel & Susanna Wesley Mr. Romley, Curate at Epworth John Taylor of Epworth William Mason, poet William Wilberforce, philanthropist	Epworth Church Wesley preaching on his father's tomb The mob at Mighton-Car Grimsby — Boston Church Lincoln Cathedral PLATE: The Docks at Hull
	MANCHESTER	
Shipston — Salford Chapel Boothbank — Davyhulme Congleton	Sir Richard Arkwright, inventor George Stephenson, engineer King Arthur	A 'knight of fame' Sir Richard Arkwright, inventor of the Spinning Jenny Peel Park

PLACES	PEOPLE	ILLUSTRATIONS
Macclesfield	Sir Launcelot of the Lake	The Royal Exchange, Market Street
Stockport	John Byrom, poet	Stephenson's 'Rocket'
	Mr. Kinchin, Fellow of Corpus	Owen's College in Oxford Street
	Mr. Hoole, Rector of St. Ann's. Christi	Oldham Street Chapel
	John Haime	PLATE: Free Trade Hall, Manchester
	Dr. Price & his views	

BRISTOL

Baldwin Street	George Whitefield	The Old Room in the Horsefair
Newgate Chapel		Pithay, Bristol
Hannam Mount, Kingswood		Maryleport Street, Bristol
Rose Green		Outdoor preaching
Lawford Gate		Bristol in the 17th Century
Kingswood School		PLATE: Bristol from St. Augustine's
		Quay
		Clifton Suspension Bridge
		Portland Square

WEST RIDING OF YORKSHIRE

Leeds — Todmorden	Daniel Defoe	The Young Pretender, 'Bonnie Prince Charlie'
Huddersfield — Haworth	William Grimshaw	Leeds in Wesley's time
Gawksham — Heptonstall	The Young Pretender, 'Bonnie Prince Charlie'	Fountains Abbey
Bingley — Otley — Bradford	John Jane	The Market Place, Huddersfield
Padiham — Clough — Colne	Dr. Smollett's History	Haworth Church & Mr. Grimshaw
Wakefield — Rothwell — Leeds	Mr. Ritchie of Otley	Studley Park
Harewood House	Mr. Wilson, vicar of Otley	Lister's Mill, Manningham, Bradford
		Mill-hands at Saltaire

WINCHESTER

Winchester Cathedral	Hedda, first Bishop of Winchester	Rufus Stirrup
Newport, Isle of Wight	King Canute — King Alfred	General view of Winchester
Southampton	William of Wykeham	High Street — Westgate, Winchester
Romsey	Bishop Edington	PLATE: High Street, Southampton
Yarmouth	Cardinal Beaufort	Brockenhurst Church
Swanage	William the Conqueror — William Rufus	Bar Gate, Southampton
	Dr. Isaac Watts, hymn-writer	Isaac Watts
		Rufus' Stone, New Forest

PLACES	PEOPLE	ILLUSTRATIONS

SCOTLAND

PLACES	PEOPLE	ILLUSTRATIONS
Old Canus — Prestonfield	William Wallace	Dumbarton Rock
Edinburgh — Holyrood-House	Robert Bruce	John Knox
Aberdeen — Murray	The Young Pretender	On the Forth
Elgin — River Spey	Ninian	Princes Street, Edinburgh
Keith — Strathbogie	Columba	Loch Clare & Ben Leagach
Fochabers	Patrick Hamilton	Holyrood Palace
Glasgow	John Knox	PLATE: Balmoral Castle
Perth	Mary Queen of Scots	King's College, Old Aberdeen
Banff		Glamis
St. Andrews		Ruins of St. Andrew's Cathedral
Dundee		Abergeldie Castle, Crattie parish
Carse of Gowry		Church, Braemar Castle
Fort-Glen		PLATE: Broomielaw Bridge, Glasgow

LIVERPOOL

PLACES	PEOPLE	ILLUSTRATIONS
Warrington	Lord Erskine	The Perch Rock Light, Liverpool
		Merseysiders boarding ship
		Liverpool, about 1755
		The Brown Free Library & Museum
		Picton Reading Room & Walker Art Gallery, Liverpool
		Strand Street & Custom House, Liverpool
		Liverpool College
		St. George's Hall, Liverpool
		PLATE: Liverpool Port

CORNWALL

PLACES	PEOPLE	ILLUSTRATIONS
St. Ives	Edward, the Black Prince	Rocks at Kynance
Falmouth	The Giant Cormoran	Cornish heath
Marazion	Admiral Lestock	Land's End
St. Michael's Mount	St. John St. Aubyn	Newlyn, with Penzance
St. Just	Edward Greenfield	St. Michael's Mount
Crowan		Falmouth
Camborne		Preaching in Gwennap Pit

PLACES	PEOPLE	ILLUSTRATIONS
Gwennap		Rocks near the Lizard
St. Agnes		Fishing boats coming home
Redruth		Wesley riding through Camborne
Bodmin — Trenuth		Polpeor — Wesley riding to St. Just
Launceston — St. Austell		Penzance

DURHAM

PLACES	PEOPLE	ILLUSTRATIONS
Lindisfarne		Durham Cathedral Door-knocker
New - Orygan	St. Cuthbert	Durham Cathedral Nave
Teesdale — Weardale	The Venerable Bede	Durham Cathedral Choir
Stockton - upon - Tees	William the Conqueror	View of Durham Cathedral & Castle
Sunderland — Darlington	William IV	Tomb of Bede, Durham Cathedral
Cuthburton — River Tees	Prior Richard de Hoton	Norman Doorway in Durham Castle
Newcastle	Bishop Hatfield	PLATE: Durham from the river
Durham Castle		Durham Cathedral from the s. west
Aycliffe		

KENT

PLACES	PEOPLE	ILLUSTRATIONS
Dover Castle		Shakespeare's Cliff, Dover
Rochester	Gregory	Charles Dickens, man of Kent
Watling Street	St. Augustine	West Gate, Canterbury
Canterbury	Charles Dickens	Country ride to Sevenoaks
Leigh — Shoreham	Voltaire	Tunbridge Wells from Mt. Ephraim
Sevenoaks — Dover		Canterbury from Harbledown
Shakespeare's Cliff		Tonbridge Castle
Bromley — Sittingbourne		Penshurst Church
Chatham — Gravesend		Ruins of Sissinghurst
Tunbridge Wells — Minster		Saluting Battery Gate, Dover Castle
Queensborough		Penshurst Place
Stroud — Margate		Rochester Castle, from the Medway

BIRMINGHAM

PLACES	PEOPLE	ILLUSTRATIONS
Edgehill - Naseby	William Shakespeare	Swords found at Edgehill, & badge of Charles I
Rugby School	Thomas Arnold	Wesley at Wednesbury
Wednesbury — Bilbrook	John Fletcher	Mill at Edgehill

PLACES	PEOPLE	ILLUSTRATIONS
Madeley	Josiah Wedgwood	The Church & Vicarage, Madeley
Wolverhampton	William Murdock	St. Martin's in the Bull Ring
Coventry — Derby	James Watt	View of 'Bermingham' - an old print
Hagley - Park	Matthew Boulton	PLATE: General view of Birmingham
The farm at Leasowes	John Leland, antiquarian	Rugby School chapel & Thomas
Stafford		Arnold, famous headmaster
Belper		Stratford views: the Free School,
		Shakespeare's birthplace
		Anne Hathaway's Cottage

IRELAND

The Black Rock		The Colleen Bawn Rock
Athlone — Dublin	St. Patrick	Statue of Edmund Burke
Kilkenny — Dunmore	Columba	Statue of Henry Grattan
Cork — Cove — Clonmel	Henry Grattan	Courtyard of Dublin Castle
Ballingarrane	Edmund Burke	PLATE: The Custom House
Ulster — Newry — Belfast	Oliver Goldsmith	Dr. Benjamin Franklin
Lisburn — Moira — Donegal	Dr. Benjamin Franklin	John Wesley at Cork
Mayo — Leitrim		Ballyshannon & the Salmon -leap
Ballyshannon — Sligo		The Lakes of Killarney
Londonderry — Limerick		The Methodist College, Belfast
Coleraine		The Linen Hall, Belfast
The Giant's Causeway		Irish factory hands

LONDON OF THE MID - 18TH CENTURY

The House of Lords		Bow Church & Cheapside
King George 11	Christopher Wren	Christopher Wren
Westminster School	William Cowper, poet	Pall Mall, about 1740
Lewisham — Tottenham Court Road	Death of Whitefield	Houses of Parliament from the river
The London Workhouse	Thomas Gray, poet	Vauxhall in 1751
Hampton Court — Moorfields	Dr. Samuel Johnson	The Monument
Bethnal Green		London Bridge before the removal
All — Hallows Church, Lombard		King George 11 of the houses
Spitalfields Street		Cornhill, the Exchange & Lombard
St. Peter's, Cornhill		Street, from an old print

PLACES	PEOPLE	ILLUSTRATIONS
Spitalfields		London shoe-black, 1750
		Hampton Court — Thomas Gray
		King George III — Handel
		Dr. Johnson meeting with John Wesley

NEWCASTLE & THE NORTH-EAST

Gateshead Fell		Wesley on Gateshead-Fell
Morpeth — Placey	King Henry II	Grainger Street, Newcastle
Greenside — Garth-Heads	The Young Pretender	The Royal Arcade, Newcastle
Scarborough		The Old Bridge, Berwick-upon-Tweed
		The Side, Newcastle

CAMBRIDGE

Trinity College	Sir Isaac Newton, scientist	King's College Chapel
Grantchester	Adam Sedgwick, geologist	Sir Isaac Newton's Statue
Bottishamlode	Byron, poet	Bridge at St. John's College
Lakenheath	Macaulay, historian	The Leys School, Cambridge
Norwich	George Herbert	Francis Bacon
Hinxworth	Francis Bacon	The Gateway, Jesus College
	Alfred Tennyson	Interior of King's College Chapel
	Wilberforce — Cromwell	
	William Pitt — Milton	
	Thomas Gray — Wordsworth	
	John Leland — Latimer	
	Thomas Fuller — Charles Simeon	
	John Fletcher	

YORK & THE BATTLEFIELDS OF ENGLAND

Beverley Minster	King Edwin	Battle souvenirs
Pocklington	Harald Hardrada	Sandside, Scarborough
St. Saviourgate Church	Earl Tostig	Micklegate Bar, York in the time
Wensleydale — Wensley	King Harold	Whitby of the Civil War
Richmond — Scarborough	William the Conqueror	Various aspects of Sheffield
Tadcaster — Staveley	David of Scotland	steel manufacture

PLACES	PEOPLE	ILLUSTRATIONS
Boroughbridge		PLATE: York Minster
Sheffield		

THE OLD BATH ROAD & THE WEST

PLACES	PEOPLE	ILLUSTRATIONS
The Castle Inn, Marlborough		Stagecoach
Brentford — Marlborough	John Wood, architect	John Wesley encounters 'Beau' Nash
Chippenham — Kingswood	'Beau' Nash	Bath, from near the Abbey Cemetery
Bristol — Collumpton		Marlborough's old Castle Inn, later
Tiverton — Shaftesbury		the Old School House
Salisbury — Isle of Purbeck		Mounds & monuments in Wiltshire:
Corfe Castle — Langton		Avebury — Silbury Hill — the
Swanage — Taunton		Devil's Den — Stonehenge
Frome — Exeter		Salisbury Cathedral
Plymouth — Paulton		Corfe Castle
Chew-Magna		The Market Place, Frome
		PLATE: Bath from Beechen Cliff
		Sir Joshua Reynolds
		Glastonbury
		Stagecoach of the period

WALES

PLACES	PEOPLE	ILLUSTRATIONS
Lanvachas		The Torrent Walk
Radnorshire	St. David	Dolgelly, Merionethshire
Montgomeryshire	William Morgan	Howell Harris
Merionethshire	Howell Harris	Harlech Castle
Bangor — Trecastle		A Welsh peasant woman
Monmouthshire		Bangor on the Dee
Brecknockshire		PLATE: The Lledr Valley
Carmarthenshire — Carmarthen		
Dala — Milford-Haven		
Houghton — Pembroke		
Oxwych — Swansea		
St. David's — Haverford		

PLACES	PEOPLE	ILLUSTRATIONS

NORWICH

PLACES	PEOPLE	ILLUSTRATIONS
Lynn	Edward the Confessor	St. Peter Mancroft
Lowestoft	King Athelstan	A general view of Norwich
Wells, — Fakenham	Wat Tyler	Norwich Market Place
Walsingham	Thomas Bilney	Nelson
	Dr. Beattie, poet	Pulls Ferry, Norwich
	John Evelyn, diarist	Walsingham Abbey

THE ENDURING THAMES

PLACES	PEOPLE	ILLUSTRATIONS
Windsor		Windsor Castle
Eton School	The Duke of Wellington	Eton's playing fields
Leith Hill	William Wordsworth	The Thames at Richmond Bridge
Burnham — Egham	Horace Walpole	South-Leigh Church
Mitcham — Dorking		High Street, Dorking
Cobham — South-Leigh		Reading, from Caversham Hill
Witney		The building of Westminster Bridge
Newbury		
Reading		PLATE: Eton School Quadrangle

THE LAST YEARS

PLACES	PEOPLE	ILLUSTRATIONS
Plymouth	Wilberforce	A parish church
Chatham		Interview between Wesley and Wilberforce
Brompton		Wesley's last sermon
Canterbury		The site of Wesley's last open-air sermon
Dover		
London		John Wesley
Wigan		
Winchelsea		
Spitalfields		